# Praise

You cannot afford to bury your head in the sand; digital transformation is inevitable. That said, it doesn't have to feel like rocket science—after all, you're not trying to reinvent the wheel. The five stages in the *Chaos by Design* framework will patiently guide you through all the applications and technical maneuvers you'll need to leverage in order to bring your business into the next decade.

**Paul L Gunn Jr | CEO, KUOG Corporation**

The times they are a changin'! If you don't want to be left behind, you better get yourself a copy of *Chaos by Design*. The authors present a highly flexible framework that will allow your company to nimbly adapt and pivot in response to all the unseen challenges ahead.

**Glenn Hopper | CFO, Sandline Discovery**

Change is difficult, inevitable, and unusual. Luckily, *Chaos by Design* is a wonderful balm for your digital transformation change pains. Offering original insight and a North Star blueprint, it'll help you get from here to there. You'll want to take a copy with you wherever you go in your career.

**Rick Yvanovich | CEO, TRG International**

These three authors have all demonstrated the 'spark' or '*Josh*' described in this book—absolutely essential for delivering digital transformation!

**Katrina Helmkamp | President & CEO, Cartus**

"There is no shortage of noise around digital transformation, but rarely is that noise news. The rhetoric rarely delves into the pragmatic steps on how to 'make sense' and 'take action' on the new opportunities that today's disruptive technologies offer. *Chaos by Design* combines an engaging, story-based approach with a flexible framework to help businesses' transition with speed and scale into relevance—all the while acknowledging that there's always more than one way 'to get there from here.'"

**– Raj Mamodia, Chairman & CEO - Brillio**

# CHAOS
# BY
# DESIGN:

## TALES OF EMPOWERMENT ON THE PATH
## TO DIGITAL TRANSFORMATION

Kader Sakkaria
Imran Karbhari
Trevor Macomber

Leaders
Press

Leaders
Press

ISBN (pbk) 978-1-63735-025-6
ISBN (e-book) 978-1-63735-024-9

Print Book Distributed by Simon & Schuster
1230 Avenue of the Americas
New York, NY 10020

Library of Congress Control Number: 2020925510

# DEDICATION

To our families. Thank you for your endless patience during every heads-down weeknight, late-to-start weekend, and interrupted vacation. We can't promise it was worth it, but we couldn't have done it without you.

~KS, IK, & TM

# CONTENTS

https://www.chaosbydesign.com/free

https://www.chaosbydesign.com/free

# PREFACE

**Digital transformation.**

What was your reaction to that term when you read it? Whatever your relationship is with the notion of digital transformation, there is one ground truth: It is imperative for all businesses everywhere in the world. Like it or not, digital transformation is happening, and there is no way to go but forward.

This book is about how to foster this transformation in multiple ways. Some of these methods are well-documented by business experts and industry analysts. Others are ignored or simply unrecognized. In that latter category, there is a "secret sauce" that we came to see as a fundamental part of any well-executed digital transformation. We will talk about that throughout this book.

\*\*\*

In 2005, David Foster Wallace addressed the graduating class at Kenyon College with a speech that is now one of his most-read pieces. In it, he argued gorgeously against "unconsciousness, the default setting, the rat race, the constant gnawing sense of having had, and lost, some infinite thing."

Wallace began with a parable:

> *There are two young fish swimming along, and*
> *they happen to meet an older fish swimming the*
> *other way who nods at them and says, "Morning,*
> *boys. How's the water?" And the two young fish*
> *swim on for a bit, and then eventually, one of*
> *them looks over at the other and goes, "What the*
> *hell is water?"*

Digitization is the water in which we are swimming.
Some business leaders are old fish who remember what
the "waterscape" looked like before it went electronic.
Others are young fish whose experience is wholly
digital.

Old fish, young fish—whatever the age—digital
business is now the norm. It's table stakes for any
company that wants to stay in the game. Any business
that has not made the jump, that has not embraced
digital transformation, will lose its seat at the table.

\*\*\*

## What is this book about?

Well, digital transformation, obviously—but ask 100
leaders to define digital transformation, and you'll get
100 different answers, so perhaps we'd better level-set
by offering our definition:

> *A journey of strategic, holistic organizational*
> *change, ultimately dedicated to optimizing the*
> *customer and/or end-user experience, which*

*requires the right leadership with the right mindset to create and cultivate a fearless culture of innovation, fail-fast attitudes, and curious, high-performing teams through a deliberate dose of chaos, creative business strategies, ongoing training, and—finally—the thoughtful application of digital tools and technologies.*

(And yes, that's a mouthful. Why do you think we had to write a whole book about the topic!)

Eagle-eyed readers will observe that, in our definition, the "digital" part of "digital transformation" doesn't step into the spotlight until the final few words. This is deliberate and as it should be. Without the right talent, culture, and mindset in place first, no amount of leading-edge technologies laden with buzzwords like "predictive analytics," "machine learning," or "artificial intelligence" will succeed in empowering your organization to disrupt—not just catch up to—your market and industry with a digital-first approach.

\*\*\*

## Who is this book for?

There's no hard and fast answer to that question. Company leaders, including executives and business unit leads, IT and product team managers, and anyone working in a company going through digital transformation (or on the verge of going through it) will all get value from this book.

In terms of what type of company this book is for, the information and methodology we go through is not aimed at a specific level of revenue or number of employees. We suggest that "cusp companies"—those that are ready to make the jump from one tier to the next—will get the most value from this book.

We *can* define the types of companies we are not targeting. This book is focused on established companies that are large enough to have separated operational functions—accounting, sales, marketing, and so on—to run the business. This generally leaves out start-ups, small companies with undifferentiated functions, and businesses that outsource large chunks of their operations.

Here's one important note: There are so many free tools out there that even bootstrapped start-ups and mom and pops could implement a lightweight digital strategy that would improve efficiency, communication, convenience, customer experience, etc. For example:

- A small-town hair salon that adopts online appointment scheduling
- A local candy shop with a digital inventory management system and a nice clean website for online ordering (see: COVID!)
- An antique shop that invests a small amount for a geotargeted SEO and paid search campaigns leading to a basic landing page to drive awareness and foot traffic to their physical store

A digital strategy (especially with free or low-cost tools) will not lead to the type of transformation that in turn leads to category or industry leadership—let alone genuine disruption—at the level this book is focused on.

Overall, any established company with sufficient revenues to dedicate resources to digital transformation can apply the insights and lessons we offer. Large companies—those falling into the $5 billion-plus revenue category—are likely to have a larger and more complex transformation to implement than small or medium companies. These enterprises may need to iterate the methodology in this book, starting with one or more pilot projects and then rolling out initiatives in an organized approach.

***

## Why this book?

There are a number of books about digital transformation on the market, many offering excellent advice and step-by-step instructions into every granular aspect of a transformation journey. Our book leans into a different philosophy by focusing more on an experience-sharing value proposition over a "problem/solution" one. Sure, we offer plenty of suggestions, tell plenty of stories, but ours is less of a "do this, get that" approach and more of an ongoing acknowledgment that there's always more than one way to get there from here.

Beyond this ideological distinction, this book differentiates itself through our recurring emphasis on a little-explored yet unquestionably critical aspect of transformation—that undefinable yet tangible quality of energy, evangelism, conviction, and leadership required to ensure that a transformation is successful beyond the standard "people, process, and technology" prerequisites of any change management.

This "X factor," the secret sauce we talked about at the start of this preface, is difficult to describe in English. It has an element of enthusiasm, though it goes beyond that. It is a hunger—perhaps an enthusiastic hunger—to make something happen, produce a certain result. This X factor is what business pundits point to in their analysis of successful entrepreneurs like Bill Gates, Oprah Winfrey, Elon Musk, and Sheryl Sandberg. They sometimes call it an "entrepreneurial spirit." This kind of energy and passion isn't limited to entrepreneurs; it can be tapped by any of us.

Not satisfied with the English language to convey this complex sentiment, we reached deep into our cultural roots (well, two-thirds of our cultural roots) to offer you the Hindi concept of *Josh*[1] ( जोश ), which can loosely be defined as "passion, zeal, enthusiasm, fervor, incandescence, life." *Josh* permeates every successful transformation journey, digital or otherwise.

At this point, you may be consciously or unconsciously trying to define *Josh* using concepts you already know, like "employee engagement." This has become a popular term among business experts over the past few years. Studies have shown that engaged employees have a direct relation to business success, and there is a load of content by various authors that offer advice and guidance about how to improve engagement. We absolutely agree that employee engagement is essential to a business in general and digital transformation specifically. And we absolutely agree that "employee engagement" is not a

---

[1]  Pronounced "jōshe".

synonym for *Josh*. Rather, it is a prerequisite. *Josh* is not experienced by disengaged or unmotivated employees. Engagement is the soil in which *Josh* sprouts. As a leader, it is not sufficient to implement strategies that improve employee engagement to foster *Josh*. You must go beyond those strategies to create an environment in which *Josh* can appear and be encouraged. We will talk about how to make that happen throughout this book.

Before we move on, there is one more ingredient we need to discuss. It is so important that it is the book's title. Chaos is a natural and predictable state in any transformation journey. It can be expressed individually, within teams and departments, or widely across an enterprise. Leaders know this, and it can be reflexive to try to anticipate and control chaos through advanced planning and what-if scenarios. Chaos can be perceived as detrimental to the success of a transformation initiative, a timewaster, something that can interfere with the plan and negatively impact the outcomes. It is considered a by-product of the uncertainty that characterizes the changes brought about by transformation. Many leaders think the right approach is to make things as certain as possible for all stakeholders. By doing this, they believe that chaos will be minimized and the initiative will benefit from it.

The truth is the exact opposite. We have participated in numerous transformation efforts, and we know up close and personal that chaos is necessary. Expressed more accurately, chaos *by design* is necessary. Rather than trying to minimize chaos, an effective transformation leader uses it productively, channeling it to fuel innovation and results. Rather than attempting to squelch uncertainty, such a leader helps employees—and the company at large—to thrive in uncertain environments. They welcome new voices to the table, knowing that a diversity of viewpoints can be chaotic in constructive ways. They emphasize adaptability, reliance on intuition, the ability to tolerate paradox, and entrepreneurial creativity to foster an agile workforce able to flourish in the presence of uncertainty and chaos.

This whole book is steeped in chaos by design, particularly as it relates to digital transformation and its impact on user experience. So, strap in, prepare yourself for new ways to think about and approach your work, and let's get started.

## Two Items of Note

1. For ease of reading, we have settled on using the collective "we" when referring to personal thoughts, recommendations, or experiences. In some cases, we may mean the pronoun literally, as the three of us have a good deal of overlapping work history in various combinations, plus a uniformity of opinion about numerous topics, which is why we collaborated on a book in the first place! Other times, "we" might refer to only one of our lived experiences, yet we have employed the conceit for consistency and to avoid the game of whose name gets mentioned more.

2. Periodically throughout the book, we will cut away to sidebars we're calling "North Star Stories." These are case studies, anecdotes, or other concrete examples that illustrate one or more concepts in the book. While they are not necessarily core to the narrative, we feel they help bring to life certain aspects of digital transformation that may not quite resonate when read at a theoretical remove. Skip or consume them at your prerogative.

# INTRODUCTION

**"We have to do this."**
We were talking to the CIO of a large insurance company, and after a pause in the conversation, he made that comment.

The "this" he was referring to was digital transformation. He needed to translate processes and procedures across the company into online and digital versions. He knew what he didn't know about taking on the task; he also knew that he didn't know what *else* he didn't know. That was why we were meeting with him.

We've had meetings like this more and more frequently over the past five years. Digital transformation has been on the minds of many executives across many business sectors for some time. But the big wave came in the spring of 2020, with the arrival of the coronavirus pandemic. Companies had to quickly pivot to virtual work, and the digital transformation initiatives that had been meandering through their organizations needed to be in place NOW.

That pivot has made a permanent shift in the way companies do business. Like the technologies that preceded it—desktop computers, local area networks, the internet, and so on—digital transformation is now part of the baseline for operations instead of being optional or off in the future. Many companies that were able to stand up "quick and dirty" digital work processes to meet the crisis must now make the transformation permanent.

We are here to help.

If your company met the COVID-19 challenge by putting digital procedures in place, it has broken through a significant barrier. Leadership in these companies may have gotten an inkling of how far behind they are. Leaders in other companies may have seen what's happening around them even before the pandemic, but they don't have the expertise or perhaps even the motivation to take on digital transformation in-house. In either case, these companies are in danger of being left behind with all the outcomes that situation brings.

It's time to jump. Ultimately, when you've gotten to the other side of this step change and look back, it will be obvious that the jump was a good thing. You'll be repositioned in your market and able to keep up if not get ahead.

One goal of this book is to give you a "macro" look at key aspects of digital transformation. We start with data gathering and clarifying current state, then move to discussing the approach that is needed to succeed. Getting your people behind the initiative—even more, sparking an experience of *Josh* in them—is a big piece of the puzzle, and we talk about some of the ways that can be accomplished. From there, we go through planning the "from here to there" path and, finally, the point where you step back, and your team gets it done. Inspired by the COVID-19 crisis so many businesses went through, we talk about "emergency proofing" your enterprise so you can quickly shift if an urgent need arises.

That all sounds very orderly and organized, doesn't it? The reality is quite different. Even the most well-executed digital transformation initiative is chaotic. As we pointed out earlier, chaos is an element of any transformation. In fact, it is one of the most predictable elements present in any type of transformation.

The good news is that the presence of chaos is a sign that things are working the way they are supposed to. Leaders can tap into the benefits of chaos when they expect it. They can monitor instability (and manage it if needed) while ultimately leveraging the "cultural entropy" it creates to adapt to new paradigms quickly despite the inevitable turmoil to their business and operations.

The purpose of this book is to help you with guiding principles, both for you as an individual and for your organization as a whole, so you can get through this journey successfully. The future is digital, and if your business isn't, it will either fail or—at best—perform well below its ultimate capabilities.

But where does the journey begin? The answer is different for every company, so before we answer in the general, let us answer in the specific by examining several transformation journeys from the outside in.

# 1

# THE 411 ON DIGITAL TRANSFORMATION

*"Digital transformation is less about a digital strategy and more about how to do business in a digital world. If we lead with technology, we're achieving digital insertion. Leading with the business outcomes ensures we are transforming."*
— Anne Mullins, CIO and
corporate vice president, Lockheed Martin

From fire to the wheel, from the assembly line to the internet, transformation has been an integral part of human history and culture. Inventor and visionary R. Buckminster Fuller noted this as he considered the timeline of discoveries and inventions from prehistory to the late twentieth century. Most relevant to this book, he also noted the noticeable acceleration of technology development from World War I onward as industry moved "from the track to the trackless, from the wire to the wireless."

This ever-increasing rate of change was naturally accompanied by transformation. And transformation. And transformation. Every business, every industry sector, has experienced multiple transformations, the kind that can't be ignored without being left behind. Some companies adapted by doing what needed to be done to stay in business. Other companies, whether slow or simply in denial, failed to adapt—or adapted too late—and fell by the wayside.

***

An example of a company that nearly missed the boat because it could not respond to market changes quickly enough is IBM. In his book, *Who Says Elephants Can't Dance?* Louis Gerstner tells the story of the transformation of the corporation from his point of view as CEO and talks about what it took to save IBM from itself.

The corporation was floundering in the early 1990s. It had stepped outside its traditions in the early 1980s with the launch of the PC, transforming the desktop computer market and the way companies around the world conducted business. Changes in the computer industry, though, had accelerated rapidly since then. By 1993, it was obvious to everyone with an eye on the industry that Big Blue was on a downhill slide.

Then Lou Gerstner happened. Wooed relentlessly, the initially reluctant Gerstner took the helm of IBM as both chairman and CEO. The date: April Fool's Day, 1993. A commonly shared assumption was that he had been brought in to oversee the death of the mammoth and see IBM carved up into separate businesses. The reality was the complete opposite.

In his book, Gerstner gives a firsthand account of IBM's transformation from an "inbred and ingrown" corporation to a competitive titan. From his point of view, the plan to cut up the company into separate businesses was a nonstarter; IBM as a whole was the way to go. Nonetheless, he took aggressive and sometimes drastic steps, cutting billions of dollars out of the expense columns and generating cash through asset sales.

Gerstner also took steps to transform the corporate culture from an inward focus to an emphasis on the customer—no easy feat. He consolidated all brand messaging into one agency, ensuring that IBM's public face would be consistent no matter what angle it was viewed from. He changed the structure of employee compensation so it was based on overall company performance rather than individual unit performance. Teamwork and speed of decisions and action were rewarded, and other compensation-based initiatives were put in place to reinforce the "all one company" and "focus on the customer" imperatives.

The result of Gerstner's tenure is evident to everyone. IBM continues to be a strong contender in its markets, and its culture is still rooted in the transformation created by the CEO of the last decade of the twentieth century.

Though the book was first published nearly twenty years ago, *Who Says Elephants Can't Dance?* is one of those evergreen stories with plenty of thought-provoking material for today's executive. If nothing else, Gerstner's story will prompt the question, "Heck, if IBM could do it, why can't we?"

\*\*\*

Microsoft has been one of the "big dogs" in the technology space for several decades. It has undergone continuous transformation: the application product path from floppy disk to DVD to cloud-based subscription is one obvious example of how the company has changed as technology has changed.

On the business-to-business (B2B) side, Bill Gates and Steve Ballmer grew the enterprise during an era when technology vendors were territorial—customers were locked in and buying a full stack of products, so the company was an IBM shop, an Oracle shop, a Microsoft shop.

Times changed. As cloud services became embedded into the technology sector, companies no longer subscribed to the monolithic strategy of having a single vendor for everything. They selected software and services based on the best fit for need, without much emphasis on vendors.

One effect of this change was a shift in power from vendor to buyer. As late as the mid-2010s, Microsoft was not positioned for this. Its culture was one of muscle-flexing, compelling enterprise customers to buy all Microsoft all the time and taking an essentially hostile posture with partners and third-party developers.

Enter Satya Nadella as CEO in 2014. Nadella understood that focus on the customer was the path to success. "It is incumbent upon us, especially those of us who are platform vendors, to partner broadly to solve real pain points our customers have," he said. Over time, he transformed the Microsoft culture into one with a customer-first focus; he also championed a collaborative approach in working with other technology enterprises.

This transformation, reminiscent of the one at IBM under Gerstner, has facilitated improvements in its offerings and put Microsoft back among the leaders in its markets.

***

Transformation is tapping companies on the shoulder once again, and this time it's affecting all industries around the globe. Digital transformation is about customer experience, and customer experience is vital to future business success.

Digital transformation is the *only* path to success. More accurately, "digital" is now the language of transformation. Like any language, it has its own grammar and associated rules. It varies from culture to culture, and even within a single company, there is nuance, idiom, and dialect. But even with variations, the language is recognizable anywhere in the world.

Like English from Old to Middle to current, the digital language has changed over time. Until the mid-1980s, computers were only in the largest businesses; they took up huge, temperature-controlled rooms. The appearance of the desktop computer, followed by local area networks followed by the internet, changed the picture and introduced the digital language to companies of all sizes. From there, a host of technological advancements has transformed industries as well as business functions like marketing, sales, and accounting.

## TransUnion: Eating Digital Transformation for Breakfast

TransUnion, the global information corporation that provides key data to businesses and consumers, has eaten digital transformation for breakfast throughout its fifty-plus years in business.

TransUnion began in 1968 as the parent holding firm for the Union Tank Car Company, a business focused on railcar leasing. The following year, after the acquisition of the Credit Bureau of Cook County, TransUnion made its first digital transformation. It was the first credit reporting business to transition to automated tape-to-disk transfer of accounts receivable information, a process that had previously been manual. This initial transformation proved valuable by significantly reducing the time and expense of updating consumer records.

Over the next two decades, Transunion continued to invest in technology and strategic growth to continuously improve its maintenance of consumer data. By its twentieth birthday the company's footprint spanned the whole United States. It expanded its services into the business-to-business space in the 1990s, followed by the launch of direct-to-consumer (B2C) offerings in the first decade of the twenty-first century. Every expansion was accompanied by digital transformation.

One key example of this was Project Spark, which transitioned its massive data assets off the mainframe computer infrastructure; the project was completed in 2016.

Today, while many consumers immediately think "credit score" when they see or hear the company name, there's much more going on at TransUnion. The company serves B2B and B2C customers across thirty countries on five continents, offering nearly 120 discrete products and solutions.

Digital transformation as a business strategy has been part of the conversation for a decade or more, but it hasn't been an imperative. Until now. Unprecedented and unexpected requirements hit businesses with the coronavirus pandemic. Suddenly, employees needed to be able to work from home, meetings and conferences had to be virtual, and business functions had to learn a whole new language to operate. Equally suddenly, companies that had been avoiding digital transformation discovered advantages to remote workforces.

The genie is not going back into the bottle. COVID-19 may have triggered the immediate need for digital transformation, but even when the pandemic is a distant memory, the digital language will remain and continue to evolve. Digital transformation is now the table stake needed to stay in the game. And like the companies of the past that didn't embrace the transformations of their times, those businesses that don't permanently embed digital into their operations will disappear from the marketplace.

COVID-19 also has affected how customers interact with businesses. As a close-to-home example for many people, who would have thought that kindergarteners would be learning from home through a computer screen? House sales, car sales, even courtroom proceedings are being managed through real-time computer interaction. In transactions that require in-person interaction—food delivery, repair people—contactless communication and payment have been implemented.

These examples of digitally supported behavior have changed customer experience and expectations. Any business focused on success must recognize this change and do whatever is needed to enable its operations and customer interfaces digitally. Failure to do this will—sooner or later—lead to failure of the business.

## No Change, No Company: the Story of Blockbuster Video

Blockbuster Video originated in 1985 with the opening of its first store. At that time, the only choice for on-demand video viewing was renting cassettes, and later DVDs, from a brick-and-mortar store. In 1987, investors entered the scene and helped to expand Blockbuster across the United States. Through an acquisition, the company also extended its market overseas. By 1992, there were 2,800 Blockbuster stores.

Giant communications corporation Viacom purchased Blockbuster in 1994. Three years later, a cheeky start-up named Netflix was founded. For a flat monthly subscription, customers rented DVDs, which they received by mail. Equally revolutionary, Netflix charged no late fees. Blockbuster realized 16 percent of its revenue via late fees at this time.

Blockbuster had a chance to continue its success but passed it up. In 2000, it could have bought Netflix for only $50 million. Company management, however, decided not to go through with the purchase. Big mistake.

Redbox, the other major challenger for the Blockbuster crown, entered the market in 2002. If research hadn't already indicated customer preferences, the popularity of Netflix and Redbox showed that consumers wanted fast rental options with no late fees. Though still the major player in the field at 9,000 stores and $5.9 billion annual revenues, Blockbuster had to make changes.

The company started Blockbuster Online and ended late fees, two resource-intensive strategies. It was too late, however, to catch up with the two younger enterprises; Blockbuster lost 75 percent of its market value between 2003 and 2005. The company declared bankruptcy in 2010 but was given a potentially new lease on life when Dish Network bought it out of bankruptcy. At that point there were 600 stores. Three years later, Dish Network announced the closing of the 300 stores still standing.

For twenty years, Blockbuster was the most popular movie rental business in the United States, dominating its market. Its inability to assimilate new technologies that fostered new customer expectations and demands was a major cause of its demise. Today there is just one (privately-owned) Blockbuster store in operation—and even that is also an Airbnb rental.

***

If you think that only certain types of companies can undertake digital transformation, think again. Along with well-touted case studies like Walmart, Domino's, and Walgreens, many firms across a variety of business sectors are pursuing digital initiatives to improve their operations and customer relationships.

**Putnam Investments,** a privately owned investment management firm, is leading the way with digital transformation in the finance sector. Moving many of its applications to the cloud, Putnam has a keen focus on data. Its data science center of excellence has incorporated machine learning to gain more granular business insights. And the company is not neglecting its customers. It relies on proven technology to continually enhance the customer experience.

**Armstrong World Industries** offers ceiling and wall solutions for commercial and residential buildings. The company's CIO streamlined business operations and leveraged transformative technologies to make the company more transparent to shareholders and develop key capabilities in analytics and cybersecurity.

**Ocean Spray,** though most often associated with cranberry bogs and apple orchards, transformed its back-office systems, focusing on robust data management to gain better insight into sales patterns and trends. Analysis includes online sales points, mobile applications and third-party websites, that offer real-time data about its products. Insight gained from its new data management practices will help the company retain customers.

> "Timely analysis and the measurement of lift and ROI can pay dividends as decisions are made on the tactical execution of different vehicles within your marketing plan."
> **–Larry Martin, Vice President,**
> **Marketing, Ocean Spray**

**Cary, North Carolina**, a town of 160,000, is leveraging the Internet of Things (IoT) and popular tools like Salesforce.com and the Amazon Echo to create a "smart city." Cary has a network of subject matter experts that includes its own citizens. While the definition of success for this digital transformation effort may shift as the town includes input from residents, smart capabilities will show up in areas like public parking, lighting, and even recycling services.

**Aspen Dental Management** is bringing its systems into the twenty-first century through the adoption of Google Cloud Platform. The huge initiative aims to increase the flexibility and nimbleness of the business and improve patient and clinician experience. A telehealth portal allows patients to video conference with their dentists, and contactless check-in has streamlined the process significantly.

**Anheuser-Busch InBev** has undergone extensive digital transformation. Among many examples, a mobile application allows retail stores to replenish orders; the app also has an algorithm that enables it to make replenishment suggestions, which is a big support for Anheuser-Busch sales reps. The company is leveraging the IoT to connect its network of breweries and monitor key metrics in each batch of brew. Artificial intelligence and machine learning also have significant roles in the company's digital footprint.

The moral of this story? You, too, can digitally transform, no matter where you sit in the business world. And we're here to show you how to pivot successfully.

# 2

## "YOU ARE HERE"

**"Let's transform!"**

Whether this call to action—or a more business-like version of it—comes from the executive suite or the head of an operational unit, it's a risky rallying cry. Transforming the organization through implementation of digital practices, processes, and policies is exciting to anticipate. It may be tempting to jump into assembling the cross-functional team and dive straight into planning. Resist the temptation.

One reason that over 70 percent of digital transformation initiatives fail is the lack of initial data gathering and baseline derivation from the data.

Many companies don't pinpoint where they are before the initiative kicks in.

To set the stage for successful transformation, organizational leaders must make haste slowly. They must focus first on gathering the data that will provide clarity around the current state of the enterprise as well as the desired outcome of the transformation initiative.

Organizations that are disciplined about tracking key information across company functions will have a relatively straightforward data gathering process.

In companies with less formal or non-standardized practices, the process can be uncomfortable for stakeholders. The activities may be like putting the company as a whole, and its administrative and operational units individually, in front of a mirror. Key stakeholders may not want to do this for fear of not liking the reflection. Managers receiving requests for data that has not been part of their metrics collection—or where there has been *no* metrics collection—may take things personally, seeing the lack of requested data as criticism of their capabilities.

This is one reason a transformation initiative must be supported at the highest level of the enterprise. *Josh*, that ineffable spark of enthusiasm that is the secret sauce of any transformation effort, must permeate the top leadership and become contagious as plans roll out to the organization. *Josh* will break through natural resistance and break the logjam preventing information collection from stakeholders.

Let's get a little more concrete here. Elon Musk founded Space Exploration Technologies Corporation, what we now call SpaceX, in the early 2000s to revolutionize space travel. His vision was the commercialization of aerospace and the ability to make space flight affordable for consumers. Since then, the company has racked up success after success and gone a long way toward realizing that vision. And the journey has been fueled by *Josh*, starting with Musk.

This is a key point. Like the distinction that exists between *Josh* and employee engagement (which we talked about in the preface), there is a distinction between vision and *Josh*. The vision is the thing the leader points to; *Josh* is what moves them to do what is necessary to get there. A visionary has a vision and experiences *Josh*. In Musk's case, an early employee of SpaceX observed that the force that drove the company's success was Musk's "enthusiasm" for space travel. We assert that this driver was more than enthusiasm—it was (and is) *Josh*.

Passion, enthusiasm, inspiration, feelings that are hard to put into words—when it comes to digital transformation, *Josh* must exist at the topmost tiers of the company. And it needs to be contagious, getting "caught" by every management level and spreading into the workforce at large.

Another aspect of executive oversight is ensuring that the data gathered and the snapshot created by that data is as honest as possible. Again, there might be resistance to this among those tasked with providing data, particularly among companies that are behind and know they are behind as well as companies that don't even realize they're behind.

The size of your company will impact the scope of the data gathering phase. For medium or large single-location companies, the effort may only need a week or two. Large firms with multiple locations or global enterprises will require more time and more complexity to gather the needed data. The latter case argues in favor of starting a digital transformation initiative with a pilot project. This allows data gathering and subsequent phases to be accomplished first in a small business unit or department. Call it a dress rehearsal for a larger initiative down the line.

An effective approach to your data gathering process is to involve key stakeholders like department managers. Tasking these stakeholders with gathering and providing data about their functional areas accomplishes two important things: You tap the people who represent the shortest route to data acquisition, and your stakeholders become invested in the process from the very beginning. We'll talk more about this in the next chapter.

## Current state picture components

To know how to get where you want to go, you need to know where you are starting. It is important to get a clear and accurate picture of the state of your organization now. External research helps understand where the company sits relative to competitors and customers. Understanding the quality of the customer experience shows what works and doesn't work in your current situation. Quantitative and qualitative metrics that make sense to your business and your industry form part of the picture; your *business capability map* and *heatmap* complete it.

External sources of data include market research, industry research, best practice and benchmarking research, and relevant information gathering. Industry analysts offer a range of information about the specific business sectors on which they focus; in the technology and IT space, Gartner, Forrester Group, and IDC are among the leading analysts. Firms including Bain, McKinsey, and Harvard Business Review also offer insight into a range of management topics. Industry associations can be valuable sources of data and information.

There is no absolute list of metrics for this exercise. The data you use will depend on your company size, the type of business you operate, and the business sector you occupy.

A business capability map is a graphic representation of the activities undertaken in each company functional area. (See page 23 for more information.) It's useful to see where duplication of effort is taking place; for example, there may be IT activities in departments outside the IT department, or more than one function may be involved in product pricing. This insight alone is worth the effort of creating the map, and it will become even more useful in planning your transformation initiative.

A heatmap follows the red-yellow-green structure familiar to many project managers and team leaders. It is constructed along two axes, the vertical listing strategic functions or capabilities (this is another place that the capabilities map is useful) and the horizontal listing logical units in the business (e.g., products, departments). The data gathered for the heatmap is used to gauge where each function or capability stands on a spectrum of zero (deep red) to 10 (deep green). The outcome gives leaders a clear picture of where things are working, where things need improvement, and where performance crises requiring immediate attention are located. (See page 27 for more information.)

An important note here. Mctrics, business capability maps, and heatmaps are needed for any organizational transformation initiative or even an audit of the organization. They are the building blocks that give leaders a clear picture of the current state of the enterprise. They also help leaders make strategic decisions and use effective levers to plan and execute the initiative. Our focus here is on *digital* transformation, but the major part of the data gathering phase is the same for similar efforts.

Another important note: As we mentioned in chapter one, you may want to pilot a digital transformation effort. Here, the data gathering and following phases we discuss will focus on the department or function you are piloting rather than the company as a whole. So, though we say "company" a lot, think about whatever organizational unit you are applying our methodology to.

Okay, enough preamble. Let's get down to it and dive into the detail for each data output.

**Metrics and all that jazz**

Metrics give you both high-level and 360-degree views of the company. They should serve as indicators for the status of important macro-aspects of the business. Companies that use a balanced scorecard to track key performance indicators (KPIs) may be ahead of the game here, as metrics that are useful for a digital transformation initiative are generally those that apply to organizational tracking in general.

We recommend that, at a minimum, you select metrics that address financial, customer service, and talent management aspects of your operations.

EBITDA—earnings before interest, taxes, depreciation, and amortization—can be a good financial metric. It is a profit indicator used by financial analysts and investors, often when valuing a company, and has been used by executives as a heuristic to gauge the company's financial status. EBITDA may not be an optimal metric for some businesses, however. For example, a retail company with high working capital requirements might not get an accurate picture using EBITDA.

If you are not already tracking an effective financial metric and are not sure EBITDA is the best measure, research what your peers are doing or what experts in your industry recommend. See if analysts in your business sector offer financial benchmark reports. As an example, Greg Herring, a strategic financial consultant serving the landscape management industry, advises his clients to use net profit margin as a key metric, and he publishes an annual benchmark report that allows company owners to calculate and compare their number with their peers.

Looking to your client base is a key metric. If you are already conducting client satisfaction surveys, you likely have a metric for this aspect of your company. If you don't have a way to generate a customer-based metric, the Net Promoter Score (NPS) is a widely accepted measure of customer satisfaction. The NPS is the percentage of customers who are promoters minus the percentage who are detractors. You can easily find online tools and instructions for generating your own NPS. Once you have this number, look for benchmarking in your industry so you can see where you stand relative to your peers.

Your talent is the last of the "big three" metrics, and, as we will discuss in much more detail later, it is critical for a transformation initiative. This metric is actually three sub-metrics that give you a picture of the "personality" of your workforce. Besides the majority of staff who keep the business running, transformation requires a small number of innovative thinkers and a slightly larger number who can advocate, influence, and support their colleagues as changes are implemented. It is important to understand the current composition of your workforce to gauge their transformation readiness.

We are big fans of the Vitality Curve used by Jack Welch when he was CEO of General Electric. We have translated his model into these ideal metrics:

A. Visionaries who can ideate outside the traditional boundaries of the company and the industry: 5 percent
B. Bridge workers who can execute on the strategies formulated by the visionaries: 10 percent
C. The employees who keep things running: 75 percent

It doesn't take a math genius to see that 10 percent is still outstanding. That could be considered group D, which are those employees who do not fit for whatever reasons and will leave or be terminated.

Measuring your ABCs is mainly a qualitative exercise that relies on the input you get from your managers. Ask your functional leads who in their staff fits each letter category (including D to get a sense of the percentage of "non-fits"). You can roll up the results into an overall distribution across the three key areas to see how ready your staff is for a transformation effort. As a side note, it wouldn't be a bad idea to get the specific names of the employees that fit in categories A and B; you may need to tap them in future phases.

## Your business capabilities map

"What do you do here?" No, we're not quoting *Office Space*. That's the fundamental question to be answered by every functional unit of the organization in order to build a business capabilities map.

If only it were as simple to answer as it was to ask. To create an accurate map of the activities and capabilities and where they reside, a much finer level of detail is needed. Think of it like a funnel, going from macro/general terms to very specific ones.

The organization chart is a good beginning. It will generate that first range of "buckets," like procurement, sales, marketing, finance, contracts, manufacturing, and other high-level functions. In the context of digital transformation, looking at peer company organizational charts can be valuable, especially those charts for companies that are engaged in or have accomplished their digital goals. The data gathered from other firms' organizational charts can be useful in the planning phase, where you could compare your chart to others to determine whether you need to restructure.

Drill down into each bucket by querying the key stakeholders, starting with that basic first question. For example, "marketing" would be the response of the marketing director to the initial question. The follow-up question might be, "How do you market?" The response might include public relations, advertising, content marketing, creation and maintenance of marketing collaterals, or social media marketing. Continuing to ask the "how" question for each area might reveal that outside contractors comprise a large part of one or more capability areas, so "contractor selection" and "contractor management" would be added to the list. You might also find there is a large technology component to marketing, like a content management system, an email campaign platform, or a social media management tool. This would add capabilities pertaining to specific tools and technology requirements.

Business capability mapping can also help see ineffective functional duplication across the company. Extending the marketing example, asking the IT lead the same questions may reveal that the capabilities needed to maintain the platforms that marketing uses also reside in IT. Should the duplication stay in place? Or is it more useful to move the capabilities to IT and create processes that connect them to marketing? There's no absolute right answer. Different solutions are best for different companies. Business capability mapping, though, has unearthed the duplication, which allows leadership to make an informed decision. You will likely see a number of duplicate capabilities or "shadow functions" as you build your map.

# Business Capabilities Map

| | Marketing | Sales and Business Development | Product and Innovation | Finance and Accounting | Technology | Operations and Account Management |
|---|---|---|---|---|---|---|
| Department or team description | Promote the business and mission of an organization. It serves as the face of the company, coordinating and producing all materials representing the business. | Engage in a variety of activities with the objective to initiate the customer purchase of a product or the client engagement of a service. | Incubate, develop, and commercialize new products and services and manage each product/service lifecycle within the overall strategic process of business lifecycle management. | Summarize financial activity in your business in the profit and loss statement, balance sheet and cash flow statement. | Provide the infrastructure for automation, implement the governance for the use of network and operating systems, and assists operational units by providing them the functionality they need. | Deliver products and services. Nurture client and customer relationships post-sales. Retain and grow business with existing clients and customers. |
| Function 1 | Brand strategy and management | Market research | Product design and planning | Accounts payable | Platform maintenance/upgrades | Managing client/customer relationships |
| Function 2 | Campaign management | Competitive intelligence | Customer success planning | Accounts receivable and revenue tracking | IT Security | Retaining existing clients/customers |
| Function 3 | Advertising | Prospect correspondance | Competitive intelligence | Payroll | Building new features | Expanding business w/existing clients/customers |
| Function 4 | Social media | Converting sales and customer acquisition | Product engineering/prototyping | Reporting and financial statements | Cross-platform development | Implementing new clients |
| Function 5 | Events | Order management | Market research | Financial controls | Public website maintenance/updates | Benchmarking |
| Function 6 | External media liaison | Email management | Client/customer surveys | Risk management | Client/customer analytics | Client/customer surveys |
| Function 7 | Customer and market research | Prospect analytics | Benchmarking | Cash flow management | Hardware maintenance | |
| Function 8 | Competitive intelligence | Expanding business w/existing clients/customers | | | Help desk | |

An important note about the tools needed to create a business capability map: You don't need specialized applications to accomplish the task. Any tool—word processor, spreadsheet, slide creator—can be used to assemble the map. More sophisticated tools can also work. The choice should be based on what works best in your particular case. Some companies don't start digitally. Instead, they use sticky notes on a bulletin board or wall to fill in the map as the data is gathered, then build a digital version once all the pieces are in place. The bottom line is that assembly of your business capability map can be accomplished with whatever planning or reporting tools you already use. One thing to keep in mind: The map is a visual tool, and you might want the option to make changes to the map during your planning process. If so, it would be most effective for the tool you use to construct the final map to be object-oriented so that the map components can be easily moved.

### Drilling Down for a Business Capability Map: an Example

Here is a scenario that illustrates the creation and use of a business capability map.

Acme Explosives Company is embarking on a digital transformation initiative to remain competitive in its markets. R.D. Runner, a fast- and forward-thinking project manager, has been assigned the initial data gathering to get things started. One piece that R.D. is creating is a business capability map that leaders can use for strategic planning.

R.D. starts by meeting with company executives. He asks for their input about what departments and functions comprise the organizations. Based on their responses, he creates a first-level document that he uses to set up meetings with the appropriate managers.

Given the nature of the company's products, one of the key departments is Risk Management. R.D. prioritizes this and meets with Y. Lee Kayotay, department manager, first thing. Together they drill down into the structure and day-to-day activities that Kayotay oversees. R.D. takes lots of notes, including the functions and capability categories that characterize the department.

Meetings with other department managers proceed, and R.D. notices a pattern. Almost every other department has at least one risk management function. Regulatory risk management, internal risk management, customer risk management, and more—the type(s) of risk being managed depends on the department.

After meetings are complete, R.D. builds the company's business capability map, tagging the risk management function wherever it shows up. He presents the map to executives. With this graphic representation, they note that risk is being managed throughout the company. Through discussion amongst themselves and the relevant managers, they centralize all risk management in the Risk Management department and restructure—which includes replacing Kayotay as manager—to more effectively connect with the departments that are risk stakeholders.

### Your heatmap

You have metrics. You have a business capability map. The last major piece of data you need is a heatmap, a visual representation of the organization's readiness for a digital transformation initiative.

The focus of the heatmap is on the critical capabilities needed for the initiative and the status of those capabilities across the relevant departments or products. Given the vertical and horizontal nature, a spreadsheet or table is the best format for the heatmap.

Your business capability map is a good reference for populating the two axes. What are essential or critical functions for digital transformation? These capabilities comprise one axis of your heatmap and should be hyper-specific to your organization.

The other axis is comprised of the products or departments that will be part of the initiative (in some cases, this will be *all* products or departments). When both axes are filled in, you have the structure of your heatmap.

The "heat" part of the heatmap reflects the status of each function in each department. The data is gathered by rounding back to meet with department leads. Using a scale of zero (an emergency) to 10 (excellent), ask the lead to assign a number that reflects their assessment of the status of each function in the vertical column. When you've made all the rounds, you will have a matrix filled with numbers. Now it's time to color!

Using this key, color each cell of the matrix according to the number entry. When complete, you have a heatmap. Below is a simple example of a heatmap focused on digital transformation.

---

\* Readers should refer to our website at www.chaosbydesign.com for full-color versions of all illustrations.

# Business Heatmap Analysis

| PRODUCTS & CAPABILITIES | Product 1 | Product 2 | Product 3 | Product 4 | Product 5 | Product 6 | Product 7 | Product 8 | Product 9 | Product 10 | TOTAL AVERAGE PER CAPABILITY |
|---|---|---|---|---|---|---|---|---|---|---|---|
| Capability 1 | 10.00 | 8.76 | 4.33 | 5.00 | 7.40 | 4.00 | 7.00 | 4.00 | 7.20 | 9.20 | 6.69 |
| Capability 2 | 8.50 | 4.00 | 7.00 | 7.90 | 6.50 | 3.50 | 3.90 | 5.50 | 7.80 | 7.60 | 6.20 |
| Capability 3 | 6.00 | 10.00 | 3.67 | 0.00 | 4.50 | 8.30 | 1.80 | 2.20 | 8.40 | 0.00 | 4.19 |
| Capability 4 | 6.00 | 7.00 | 9.00 | 4.67 | 4.00 | 3.67 | 1.00 | 6.50 | 1.50 | 4.00 | 4.93 |
| Capability 5 | 3.00 | 4.00 | 8.50 | 6.90 | 3.00 | 8.80 | 6.00 | 7.90 | 3.60 | 6.50 | 5.73 |
| Capability 6 | 3.80 | 4.20 | 5.20 | 6.00 | 4.20 | 2.80 | 3.80 | 4.20 | 9.20 | 8.60 | 4.40 |
| TOTAL AVERAGE PER PRODUCT | 6.47 | 6.16 | 9.95 | 4.08 | 4.43 | 4.01 | 4.60 | 1.25 | 5.45 | 5.37 | 5.36 |

Rankings   10.0   8.0   5.0   3.0   0.0

The heatmap offers an easy-to-read picture of the company's transformation readiness (or lack of readiness). Executives can pinpoint where improvements must be made and where things are in good shape to proceed.

### Data is king

Whether focusing on a smaller pilot or planning a cross-company initiative, the information you gather in this first phase is crucial. The metrics, business capability map, and heatmap form the baseline for the initiative. They create a snapshot of the current state of the company relative to digital transformation. Analyzing this data, an exercise we will talk about later, will support initiative planning. Future data gathering efforts can track progress, improvement, and status of the initiative.

---

\* Readers should refer to our website at www.chaosbydesign.com for full-color versions of all illustrations.

# 3

# THE ART OF THE POSSIBLE

*"We choose to go to the moon in this decade and do the other things, not because they are easy, but because they are hard, because that goal will serve to organize and measure the best of our energies and skills, because that challenge is one that we are willing to accept, one we are unwilling to postpone, and one which we intend to win...Space is there, and we're going to climb it, and the moon and the planets are there, and new hopes for knowledge and peace are there. And, therefore, as we set sail, we ask God's blessing on the most hazardous and dangerous and greatest adventure on which man has ever embarked."*

These excerpts are from a famous speech delivered by President John F. Kennedy in 1962, announcing the goal of putting a man on the moon within the decade. This speech pointed to what was possible and set a North Star for the United States. The stories of the people who followed that star and accomplished the goal are now legend.

Kennedy's mandate is a great illustration of the need for *Josh* from the top. JFK created *Josh* in all the organizations involved in the undertaking as well as in the public at large. And chaos—that companion of transformation—was present at every step. There are books and movies around now that show us what the experience was like, and consistent with our digital transformation experience, a degree of chaos attended the accomplishment.

## The Moon as the North Star

At the start of the 1960s, the United States lagged behind its most prominent competitor, the Soviet Union, in space travel. The Soviet Union had been the first to land unmanned space vehicles on the moon, and though the US did likewise, it was stuck in catch-up mode as its competitor set the path forward.

US "CEO" John Kennedy realized that the country needed to become a leader in this "market space" (yes, pun intended); further, he needed to set a goal, a North Star, that would rally everyone from scientists and engineers to farmers and storekeepers. His choice: To land a human on the moon and to be the first to do so. This was not simply traveling into space. This was a specific goal and a very big one—in the language of goal-setting, it was a high, hard goal. It was, in other words, a North Star.

His first move was to get the buy-in of his "executives"—the US Congress. In 1961, he addressed a special joint session of Congress and said, "I believe this nation should commit itself to achieving the goal, before this decade is out, of landing a man on the moon and returning him safely to Earth." Kennedy got the executive support he sought, and the initiative was on.

The first step on the path to the North Star was unmanned missions to the moon. The Pioneer program had been in place since 1958, but all but one of its missions failed, and even the one that didn't was only a partial success. Ranger, the next program, started in 1961. Its initial missions were also failures. NASA staff learned from each failure and made successive corrections and improvements. The last three missions of the Ranger program (1964-65) succeeded. Its successor, Surveyor, had many more successes than failures in its missions; the vehicles in the program returned thousands of photos of the moon landscape after a series of soft landings.

Manned missions paralleled the unmanned missions. Project Mercury achieved its goal of orbiting a human around the Earth in 1962. Gemini's objectives were to master advanced space travel tasks that would enable Project Apollo, the program targeted to a human moon landing. In-space vehicle docking and the first space-walk occurred as part of Project Gemini.

These programs, manned and unmanned, led to the Apollo Program. This was the achievement of the North Star—crewed missions to the surface of the moon. The first person to step foot on the moon took place as part of Apollo 11 on July 20, 1969 reaching Kennedy's North Star. This achievement was followed by further missions.

The Apollo Program suffered two major failures: The launchpad fire of Apollo 1 and the in-space explosion of Apollo 13. Though tragic loss of life was unavoidable in the first case, the mission's Earth team members and the astronauts themselves worked together to prevent a disaster.

Besides realizing the goal set by its "CEO," the "company" known as the United States saw many benefits from the innovations, developments, and achievements of the people who were part of the program. Much of the technology environment in which we live and work today owes its roots to the digital transformation of NASA in the 1960s.

This part of the US space program, full of *Josh* and chaos, is an excellent metaphor for a company's digital transformation initiative.

## Create your North Star

Steve Case, co-founder of America Online, said, "If you're doing something new, you've got to have a vision. You've got to have a perspective. You've got to have some North Star you're aiming for, and you just believe somehow you'll get there, which kind of gets to the passion point."

The leader of an enterprise creates the North Star that will lead to transformation. Once that goal is created, the message about the North Star—the one that, like Kennedy's message, will motivate and inspire—must be crafted. This communication is vital to form the fertile ground from which the transformation initiative will grow. If there are great quotable bits in the message, all the better!

The executive team is the first tier to which the leader must deliver the message. This is not a "Hey, I want to share this vision" communication; it must create *Josh* in the senior team and empower them to pass that enthusiasm along. From there, if successful, the message takes on a life of its own as it cascades throughout the company. How that cascade looks depends on the company.

When we joined Cartus—the industry's leading corporate relocation and global talent mobility firm—the company had just begun its long-percolating digital transformation in earnest. The new CEO and CIO had already established Cartus' North Star, which we will paraphrase here as "To create a smarter, more intuitive, and more customer-centric digital experience across all products and services." We were hired to help harness the powerful and positive chaos that this new North Star had generated and spread its gospel through the ranks of the executive leadership team and beyond.

We spearheaded a "roadshow" to teams that spanned the globe. Shanghai, Hong Kong, Singapore, the United Kingdom, and on from there—we visited each team to deliver the North Star message. As a result, company employees understood the goal, the strategy, and the thought processes that led to the initiative. We moved on to presenting to clients and prospects, leveraging that all-important spirit of *Josh* to sell the experience and generate enthusiasm for the benefits they would see as a result of the specific products that Cartus' digital transformation would soon spawn.

## Harvest and reinvest to fuel the journey

Engaging in the art of the possible—sparking innovation and creativity—requires strategic practicalities. Without adequate resources, for example, navigation by the North Star will be difficult, if not impossible.

One strategy to gather sufficient resources for your digital transformation is "harvest and reinvest." This approach is common to investors when they collect the profits from investments to fund a new investment. In a company, the harvest and reinvest strategy focuses on making changes that free up finances and other resources. Implementing the strategy allows the company to fund the transformation initiative from its own resources.

Harvesting is synonymous with lowering costs. For example, one way to lower costs and reap savings is process automation. Consider what processes can be automated in your company without re-engineering or incurring additional costs. If your operating cost is a million dollars and you save $100k through automation, that's $100k that can be allocated to transformation efforts.

Another option is to engage service providers who offer SLA-based managed services for functions within your company. For example, when we joined Cartus,

the majority of our technology vendors had a time-
and material-based (T&M) contract. We converted
the vendors to outcome-based contracts to drive home
the point that our successes needed to be mutual—this
was a joint venture. If we need to release twenty new
features in the next sprint and you help us deliver them,
you earn the full value. Otherwise, the contract triggers
a diminishing return. We didn't fire anyone, and we
didn't hire any new people. These were the same teams
managing the same vendors. However, now we could
reap recurring long-term gains either in productivity,
cost savings, or both.

Consolidation of outside contractors can also yield
significant savings. For example, at TransUnion, we
participated in a big harvest and reinvest strategy that
generated $20 million in savings that was reinvested into
transformation initiatives. With focus on operational
efficiencies, we created savings by consolidating all
cell phone contracts into one provider ($1 million in
savings) and reducing the number of vendors from 130
down to six ($5 million in savings).

We use the word "savings" for convenience, but
remember that organizations shouldn't literally save
the money they harvest. Rather, think of it as adding
money to a cash register, not a savings account. In the
former instance, the capital will continue to flow in and
out of the company, funding strategic and operational
expenses; in the latter, it will sit and gather digital dust
with no tangible long-term impact.

The harvest and reinvest strategy produces a
beneficial side effect by improving efficiencies and
streamlining operations in the company. In addition,

if managed effectively, it can help the shift to a product mindset—an essential for digital transformation success. It also prepares employees for the changes related to digital transformation. The trifecta—generating resources, improving operational efficiency, and reinforcing the right culture—makes harvest and reinvest a winning approach for diving deep into the art of possible.

## The all-important product mindset

Our experience has revealed one essential culture change that needs to take place for the art of the possible to show up. This is the shift from a *project* **mindset** to a *product* **mindset**.

Until the early 2000s, companies thought in terms of projects. You pick up a project, you work on it for some length of time, and you finish it. This approach built many large and successful corporations, but the times have changed.

One of the biggest problems with this approach was that everyone moved on to the next one once the project was over. No one looked back to assess what happened in that project. What impact did it have? Can we continue to improve it? How did the beneficiaries of the project feel about it? What feedback had been gathered? Those satellite ideas died as soon as the project was complete.

Another factor in many industries was that the majority of projects never got finished, especially if they were multimillion-dollar, multiyear initiatives. A variety of changes impacted the projects. People moved in and out of the team, the strategic focus changed, leadership changed, or the key people working on the project changed. The bottom line was that the project mindset did not produce the desired outcomes.

Perhaps the most critical issue with the project mindset is that it does not include the ultimate customer experience in its approach. It focuses on the delivery of objectives with no sort of customer feedback loop. The lack of insight into customer experience precludes adjustment in the objective or goal and can affect the impact of the objective or goal once it is achieved.

Over the last decade or so, especially after the inception of agile development[1], the product mindset concept took hold. It was reinforced after the rise of newer technology-oriented organizations across industries— Facebook, Uber, and others. These enterprises introduced the product mindset, which shifted focus to the customer. Everything revolves around the customer: How do we make sure that everything we do helps support and enhance the customer and their journey?

A product mindset prompts questions like, "What is the product? Why are we creating it? What is the product's intended purpose? Who is the customer for the product?" Asking these questions early, often, and of diverse groups of employees will introduce an element of chaos that can help focus the initiative. Use answers to questions like these to build the development team, and you will have a product-oriented group from day

---

[1] Agile development can be defined as the early and continuous delivery of working software whose incremental, user-centric improvement process encourages flexible responses to change.

one. You will also instill a *question-everything* instinct that stays in the team members' minds: "How well did the product function? Can it be improved? Is it serving customer needs?"

You will know that your culture has moved to a product mindset when you hear people say things like, "We can deliver this product/feature based on what we have…" rather than "Based on these dollars and these resources, we can deliver this product/feature…" Switching the lens to the customer, focusing on what they need, makes the transformation journey easier. A further sign that a product mindset is taking hold is *Josh*. You will see enthusiasm, inspiration, innovative ideas, eagerness for the work. That is *Josh*—the indispensable factor in digital transformation.

| PRODUCT | vs. | PROJECT |
| --- | --- | --- |
| outcomes | | outputs |
| continuous value | | scope, time, budget |
| concrete (an actual thing) | | abstract (work management) |
| adaptive | | predictive |
| ongoing | | has a finish |
| value drives investment | | investments promise ROI |

An anecdotal example of a product mindset applied within a company is from the Steve Jobs Library of Stories. Back in the day, a market wrestling match was going on between Java and OpenDoc. Java was considered technologically superior, but OpenDoc still had its adherents. One of them was Steve Jobs.

Jobs was asked, "You're a big technology guy. Why the heck are you using OpenDoc?"

Jobs said, "I don't care how powerful Java is. What I care about is what my people need; OpenDoc delivers what my people need."

Jobs' response is the product mindset at work.

A product mindset starts with the desired outcome for the customer, not the solution. Jobs wasn't interested in the solution—"Everybody knows Java is the best." He was interested in what his people—his customers, in this case—needed.

Thinking about the desired outcome may seem like a no-brainer, but many companies start with a solution and then go looking for the problem it solves. This is part of a project mindset. Too often, the solution is unproven with respect to market need or, only slightly better, improperly scoped. Firms in the tech sector are especially prone to the solution-focused "Field of Dreams" approach to creating offerings for their markets: "Look at this awesome technology! Let's go sell it! If we build it, they will come!" This is where many failures happen.

Project thinking is about focusing on the solution and then figuring out how to fit it into the market. The product mindset focus is on customer experience: "I want to know what my customer wants to experience, what experience they're looking for, and I want to build something to enable that experience." Basically, you want people to talk about the outcome customers are looking for rather than the problems they are dealing with.

There are two options for embedding a product mindset into the workforce:

1. **Bottom-up.** Train teams to move a product-centered idea to a prototype in a matter of weeks using design thinking and agile methodology.

Showcase these results to the company, talk about how this was accomplished, and start getting buy-in.

2. **Top-down.** Mandate new processes and procedures by executives and other leaders.

In the context of digital transformation, the first strategy is preferable to the second by a long shot. A mandate can prompt resentment, unwillingness, and lack of buy-in by employees. It may be heard as "Do this or you're out of here," which is not constructive. The first strategy encourages the sense of ownership by employees that is so important to the success of transformation. The "mandate" comes from the floor, so to speak.

## Instill design thinking

Design thinking, an adjunct to the product mindset, is characterized by a three-prong approach: desirability, viability, and feasibility.

- Desirability is what the user or customer wants. Whether the product is an application, a toy, a car, or a productivity tool for their job, the user is looking for something.
- Viability is what technology can provide. This will vary according to the product.
- Feasibility is about the business. Can the business be successful with the product given the resources at its disposal?

Introducing design thinking into your company involves clarifying these three prongs. It can be done in several ways.

Here is yet another Steve Jobs-related story, this one illustrating how design thinking works relating to an actual product. In the first decade of this century, mobile phone designers were all about styluses. This was a holdover from some of the personal assistant devices that were operated through small pen-shaped tools. In his introduction of the first iPhone in 2007, Jobs made it crystal clear that he was staunchly anti-stylus.

"Who wants a stylus?" he said. "You have to get 'em, put 'em away, you lose 'em. Yuck! Nobody wants a stylus."

Apple didn't simply omit styluses with their new phone. The company introduced capacitive touchscreen technology. Unlike the resistive touchscreens of handheld devices up to this point, the iPhone screen could be navigated using a finger. Resistive touchscreens did not work well with a finger, which is why styluses were necessary.

"God gave us ten styluses," Jobs said. "Let's not invent another." His determination to ditch the stylus was a technology disruptor, driving previous winners in the space into obscurity and opening the door to new products and companies to step in.

This is a great illustration of design thinking founded on a product mindset. Eliminating the need for a stylus was, without question, a **desirable** feature of the new phone. The technology needed to create the resistive screen was **viable**, while Jobs' "no stylus" mandate made viability a necessity. Feasibility? This was a corporation with the resources and market insight to verify **feasibility**.

---

**Benefits Builder: Design Thinking, Up Close**

Cartus is a company that specializes in employee relocation and global talent mobility. It has a reputation for personalized service in helping employees and their families with all the pieces that comprise a move.

When we joined Cartus, clients across the relocation industry were just beginning to adopt a new program known as "core/flex." Instead of developing different policies for each move type (e.g., domestic transferee, short-term assignee, long-term assignee) and/or employee tier (e.g., new hire, entry-level, manager, executive), companies can create a single program designed around a core benefit structure while empowering employees to choose the flexible options that work best for them and their families.

While Cartus had been managing variations on this general policy approach for years, they had only recently built and piloted a digital prototype to make the process easier and more efficient for transferees, clients, and Cartus staff. After pausing development of this core/flex prototype to shift focus to a new flagship product—their single source of truth relocation platform—we received the go-ahead to return the team's attention to this growing market need. As a bonus, thanks to our previous pivot, we could build this next-generation core/flex solution directly into Cartus' new centralized mobility hub rather than keeping it as a standalone tool.

Applying a product mindset and design thinking, we streamlined many business processes within Cartus as we re-envisioned and then reengineered Cartus' core/flex solution from the ground up in less than ten months. The North Star was a flexible, points- or currency-based approach that offered relocating employees choice and control during their move while enabling clients to manage relocation budgets more precisely.

Since going live, we estimate that 70 percent of Cartus clients have expressed interest in moving to this model at some point, in whole or in part—a prime example of how even established industry leaders can continue to play the role of disruptor when focused on delivering the ultimate customer experience.

From the beginning, we enjoyed the support of cross-functional teams with representatives from every department in the company—supply chain, IT, operations, client services, and even marketing, to name a few. In addition to getting input from employees with diverse expertise during the design phase, people who rarely had access to a product until design was complete were included from the get-go.

We took the team through the entire design thinking process. No computers. Members spent weeks in conference rooms writing on sticky notes. There were complexities to work through, such as the definition of the services that transferees would want to have access to. The team also considered the relocation policies that different companies follow. With over 500 business clients, each with their own policies, Cartus manages thousands of policies. The new product had to accommodate these policies.

Or did it?

We challenged the need to manage policies. "Why manage to a policy? All we need to do is provide the list of services and let the user decide which they need. We don't need to tell them what they get." This was outside the norm of the company at that time—design thinking for the win.

Benefits Builder, the product that resulted from this effort, is now an integral part of the Cartus service portfolio. It not only created a great addition to the company's offering, it evangelized design thinking and product mindset across the workforce.

Design thinking does not have to be connected to a product or object. It can be used any time a desired outcome is established. For example, we embedded design thinking in our team through our meetings. We said, "We need to talk to each other. Information comes to us from executives and from other corners of the business that needs to make its way to you. How do you want to know what you need to know?" The team decided that they wanted daily briefings.

Our team was the user. Instead of blindly implementing a solution, we asked our users what they wanted. Based on their response, we sent them a short email every morning that conveyed information we had received.

Embedding design thinking into the company culture means that the three simple ideas of desirability, viability, and feasibility are routinely applied to reach any desired outcome.

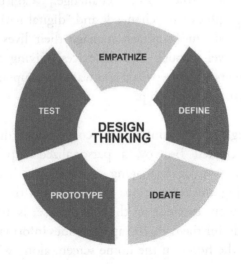

## Big Dog, New Tricks

Design thinking is not limited to young companies. Marriott International made a "from the ground up" change to its mobile application that was rooted in design thinking. Despite its position as the largest hotel chain in the world—the corporation operates 30 brands—its market is furiously competitive.

Gone are the days of telephone reservations. Even more, gone are the days when hotels and motels were the primary accommodation choice for consumers. With upstarts like Airbnb, VRBO, and HomeAway firmly embedded in the market, an already competitive landscape has become even more challenging for attracting customers.

This isn't the only challenge. Consumer demographics have changed, and "digital natives," millennials and younger, manage their lives and their travel through digital devices. Giving these customers what they need and want was imperative for Marriott leadership.

Through design thinking, the corporation's digital team created Bonvoy, a personalized app that doesn't stop at managing reservations. Besides accessing any reservations made through the app, the content expands on the day the user is due to check in for the trip. The app provides information about the hotel on the home screen, along with a map, directions, and buttons for checking in and making service requests once in the room.

Bonvoy is an excellent example of product mindset plus design thinking keeping an "old" corporation relevant and desirable in its market.

# 4

# CAPTURING HEARTS AND MINDS

As we pointed out in chapter 2, incomplete data gathering is one reason that digital transformation initiatives don't achieve desired goals. Another reason is the big "C" that every executive, leader, or any professional should pay attention to: Culture.

Technology alone will not make digital transformation successful. Culture is critical. The organization must exist in an environment that is "transformation friendly." Without a culture that welcomes and adapts to change, the most advanced technologies in the world won't matter.

Culture has to change before technology can change. *Josh* must be fostered throughout the organization. However, many leaders overlook this fact, attempting to digitize operations in a culture that is not aligned. A digital transformation effort needs to be planted in fertile ground, and that fertile ground is culture. Without a culture that supports strategy, the initiative is highly likely to fail. Culture change must be put into play before the transformation initiative is announced.

\*\*\*

Peter Drucker, expert on all things "change," wrote, "An organization must be organized for constant change." Other pundits have talked about the need to "eat change for breakfast" while pointing to the ever-accelerating rate of change. Among all the wise words about how enterprises today must embrace change, one aspect is rarely confronted head on: any change causes upset.

It doesn't matter whether it's "good" or "bad" change. Wedding, graduation, new baby—these are examples of what we tend to think of as "good" changes. There is invariably some anxiety and stress that comes along with the happiness. The same thing is true in the office. A promotion, a big sale, being assigned a plum project—these are all great, right? Sure, but those events also bring stress (What are my new responsibilities? Will I be able to do them right?), anxiety (What if my work hours extend? How will that affect my relationship/family?), and even fear (What if I fail? What if I'm fired?).

Digital transformation is change. Change causes chaos, at least initially. Ergo, digital transformation causes chaos, at least initially. And one more trite saying: Knowledge is power. Knowing that upset is likely to waft throughout the workforce once the initiative is announced allows proactive moves to change the organization's culture—to capture hearts and minds.

Capturing hearts and minds must begin before the transformation project is officially and publicly announced. The way to prepare for the big change is to pave the way with small changes. Making well-planned small changes also facilitate that all-important culture change that must precede the digital transformation effort.

## Clearly set and point to the North Star

Your North Star is a key element for capturing hearts and minds. President John F. Kennedy accomplished this with his "man on the moon" speech. From there, effective strategies, deployment of the right people, and continuing communication turned that (literally) far-off goal into a reality.

## Tap champions and connectors

You have characterized your digital transformation plan. You understand the value it offers to the company, and you understand the potential challenges or obstacles. You have *Josh*, and you have spread it to the organization's leaders. It is now time to tap the influencers in your company and pass your *Josh* along to them. They will, in turn, pass it along and help your employees understand and embrace your initiative.

Identify champions in each functional area—a finance champion, a supply chain champion, and so on. Pull this small team together and present your plan. Answer their questions. Allow them to make suggestions and act on this input. The team's involvement upfront will strengthen their sense of ownership, which will enhance their effectiveness as champions.

Next, locate the "connectors" in your company—the people with far-reaching networks that span departments and functions. Bring them together with the champions and share the transformation plan, what it will mean to work processes, and how it will benefit the firm.

The goal of your champions and connectors is to generate excitement around the transformation journey before the journey itself begins. The team's communication and responses to questions from colleagues will produce a ripple effect across the organization. Employees will get a "soft" introduction to the transformation, as opposed to official announcements from you, through your champion/connector team. The soft introduction prepares for the coming changes and allows time for employees to readjust their thinking.

Create a communication conduit that connects you with your champions and connectors. You keep them up to date on the initiative so they can spread the (accurate) word to the employees. The communication conduit will also allow your team to let you know about the sentiments and questions they encounter, which lets you "take the pulse" of the staff as you proceed through the transformation project.

**Align incentives**
One pragmatic change is to create or shift incentives that are better-aligned with the coming transformation. The message that goes with the project going public needs to be something like: "If you are part of this, if you constantly connect with it and plow through it, you're going to be rewarded."

When thinking about incentives, avoid department/ information silos. For example, say you tell your sales team, "You're going to get a commission when you sell." All they are going to do is sell, sell, sell because they're going to make a commission, commission, commission. Then you turn to the delivery team and tell them, "You'll get a bonus if you meet your delivery goal," and all they will focus on is delivery.

It soon becomes evident that having the sales team incentivized to sell and the delivery team incentivized to deliver is not in line with your strategy. Too often, what the sales team sells, the delivery team can't deliver within their goals. Given the incentives you've set in place, the sales side doesn't care one way or the other if what they sell can be delivered effectively. All that team cares about is sell, sell, sell.

You must incentivize your teams so the results support rather than impede strategic success. In this example, the solution is to more narrowly define the sales team incentive: "You're going to sell anything that can be successfully delivered and that maintains X margin."

In the blink of an eye, your sales team will shift focus to partnering with the delivery team. "What do you want to do? How can you do it? Can you do this better? How do I manage my margin?" The personal gains received from meeting the requirements now line up with expanding focus to include team partnership.

Financial incentives are the usual go-to's for leadership. But different people are motivated by different things. Some want financial gain, sure. Others are spurred by a title or the ability to leverage their experience on the project to advance their careers. Public recognition is another strong motivator.

It is important that the C-suite understands the variety of motivators in their employee population and develops the right incentives. Seek input from the HR team, as they often have a clear view of workplace motivators.

A note about changing incentives: Because of the nature of this change, it is an area that will be rife with chaos at the beginning. It will show itself in a variety of ways, like passive or very vocal resistance. As time goes on, though, the chaotic will simply become the normal.

## Use strategic silence

Silence from the company leader is not highly recommended. Usually. For capturing hearts and minds for a transformation initiative, *strategic* silence can be effective.

Consider this scenario:

A new CXO[2] comes on board. It's an overt demonstration that things are about to change, and people are waiting for them to start. For the first two, three, maybe four weeks, the CXO says nothing definitive to the staff. Suddenly there is tension growing as expectations heighten.

---

[2]  CEO, CIO, CTO—it could be anyone in the C-suite ultimately tasked with driving the transformation.

Finally, the day comes. The CXO and other executives swoop in and unveil the grand vision. If done effectively, this dispels the tension while retaining the excitement, which is now positive and affirming rather than negative and fearful.

This is strategic silence. The CXO has generated excitement and a groundswell of curiosity—both positive and negative—because answers were not forthcoming off the bat.

## Create intentional chaos

The CXO and high-level managers can also create a buzz by attending random unannounced meetings throughout the company. This can help them gain beneficial and perhaps unexpected insights from the "feet on the ground" related to the transformation. The tactic can also create "internal chaos," where people start asking, "Who is this person, why are they in this meeting, and why aren't they necessarily even saying anything or contributing?" A ripple effect of conjecture can take place throughout the company, again generating excitement and curiosity.

## Use the 80:20 Rule

A common ratio applied to a variety of business scenarios, the 80:20 Rule, applies to the composition of your transformation team. Your existing employees are the 80 percent. These people understand the company and its business. The 20 percent comprises new employees, people who come in with fresh eyes and no history. This combination connects "who we are today" to "what we will be in the future."

## Apply agile fundamentals to encourage thinking outside the box

Take employees through training that teaches them agile processes and help them incorporate the processes into their work routines. Familiarize them with the use of personas[3] to enhance their product mindset, regardless of where they sit in the company.

These actions will facilitate adoption of the transformation by everyone in the organization. Each employee will get behind the change effort because there is a personal reward to be gained—and that personal reward will differ from person to person.

## Account for minicultures

Another aspect of culture is the diversity of cultures that make up your workforce. Call them "minicultures." We are all a product of different backgrounds—familial, socioeconomic, ethnic, environmental, political—and our approach to change can vary. Keep this in mind so you do not mistake politeness for buy-in.

This anecdote helps illustrate one aspect of certain cultures:

Your neighbor knocks on the door and asks if they can borrow a cup of sugar. They are baking and have unexpectedly run out of this ingredient. You

---

[3] Personas can be thought of as fictional, broadly defined characters created to represent your potential customers or audience, who might use a software or product in a particular way.

go to your kitchen, come back, and hand them a
cup of honey (which won't work for them). You
are trying to be helpful by providing something
analogous instead of simply responding, "No, I'm
sorry. I don't have any sugar."

Though it is better to say "no" to the initial request,
you have been raised to avoid such a direct negative.
The result is that you have wasted your time and that
of your neighbor to provide something that didn't
meet the expressed need. The solution is to transcend
your upbringing and learn to say no when that is the
accurate response. And you need to learn how to say no
at the beginning before you waste your time and your
neighbor's time on resources that don't meet either side's
needs.

This is a simple example of a cultural element that
may be in place in some of your employees. Saying "no"
is almost taboo. Any other answer is preferred, and the
more positive, the better. In many Asian and Indian
cultures, for example, it is frowned upon to say no the
first time around, even if that is clearly the best approach.

This example of a culture-driven behavior can
mislead management regarding the status of the
transformation initiative. In addition, if something
is about to go off track, it may not be acknowledged,
especially if it's important to get the issue into the open,
even if there are negative aspects to the situation.

By understanding the minicultures within your
organizational culture, you can account for behaviors
that might obscure issues that come up during the
transformation initiative.

## Build consensus

There will be resistance to the change, and people will express that resistance in different ways. You, along with your champions and connectors, must focus on doing and saying what is needed to build consensus. This means "meeting people where they're at" and addressing specific issues or complaints to break through the resistance. Listen to the resistance, understand the biases and assumptions, and address them to achieve a breakthrough and build consensus.

---

### Profile in Consensus-Building: *12 Angry Men*

Consensus-building is a critical element of capturing hearts and minds. We often use the movie *12 Angry Men* to illustrate the obstacles and behaviors characteristic of the change effort that attends a digital transformation initiative. The classic 1957 film is worth a watch; here's a synopsis with a little commentary by us.

Twelve jurors have assembled to deliberate after hearing the trial of a young man accused of killing his father. It looks like a cut-and-dried case. The defendant, known to have violent tendencies, was heard to threaten his father by one neighbor, while another neighbor testified that she saw him stab his father from her window. The switchblade found at the murder scene—wiped clean of fingerprints— was the same make as the one the defendant had recently purchased.

The *fait accompli* attitude of the jurors is obvious, and the foreman calls for the vote in full expectation of unanimity. However, though eleven jurors vote guilty, Juror eight votes not guilty. When confronted about his recalcitrance, he says that he believes some discussion is needed before another vote is taken.

Juror eight details his concerns. He is skeptical about the reliability of the witnesses and also asserts that the murder weapon is a very common switchblade model. He pulls a blade of the same make out of his pocket. (Things were certainly different in the fifties!) He concludes by saying that he believes there is enough reasonable doubt about the guilt of the defendant to prevent him from voting guilty.

At his suggestion, the foreman conducts a secret vote from which Juror eight abstains. If the vote is unanimous, Juror eight promises he will vote guilty. Juror nine, however, has changed his vote, saying he also believes that more discussion is warranted.

As the film proceeds, Juror eight makes cogent points that support his doubt about the witness testimonies. One by one, other jurors change their votes, eventually infuriating hyper-resistant Juror three. Discussion turns to the actual mechanics of the stabbing, finally demonstrating that the nature of the wound makes it unlikely if not impossible that the defendant was the murderer.

One by one, the jurors change their votes. Each has a different reason for coming around to Juror eight's view, including Juror seven, who had made it clear he just wanted to get this over with and leave. At one point, Juror twelve reverts back to a guilty vote, while Juror three continues to remain convinced of the defendant's guilt.

In the end, only Juror three is left voting guilty. He is brought to the point of rage before he breaks down over the bad relationship he has with his own son. Finally, he mutters his not guilty vote, making the decision unanimous.

The film is a brilliant demonstration of how different people approach decisions and how resistant some can be to change. It also shows how consensus can be built to include even the most stubborn status-quo seekers.

Juror eight challenges the biases in the other jurors that lead to unexamined assumptions. Each individual has a different set of biases and assumptions, and Juror eight, along with other jurors after they have changed their minds, breaks through resistance one person at a time. You and your team need to be Juror eight for digital transformation.

***

You've defined the North Star and shared it through leadership levels. The human resource function is your partner in executing the pre-transformation actions.

You've also shared the North Star with your champion/connector team, and they have begun engaging with employees about the upcoming transformation initiative. Incentive programs have been modified, and the cultural mindset has shifted to an agile product focus. Sales is no longer solely focused on their narrow window of selling, marketing isn't solely focused on their piece; everyone feels connected to everyone else, and they all have a mutual incentive versus their traditionally narrow incentives.

You are prepared. It's time to officially announce the initiative.

And it's also time to play whack-a-mole.

Issues will crop up. Resistance will ooze out here and there. Rumors will circulate. Leadership's role is to resolve issues, break through resistance, and offer open and honest communication to dispel inaccurate information.

Fear will also accompany the transformation. This is one reason why establishing a product mindset before beginning the initiative is important. Fear is associated with risk, specifically risk of failing.

In managing the transformation, you will need to take certain risks. Traditional organizations are risk-averse, because that's how they've grown and succeeded; that's how all of their operations and procedures are oriented. Often the first assessment these organizations perform is a risk assessment; the outcome of the assessment has a strong influence on decision making.

The product mindset promotes, even cherishes, risk: "Fail fast" is an operating motto. If you don't remove the fear, your people won't take risks, and they won't fail fast. Failing, then using customer feedback to loop back with a different approach, is built into the product mindset. Failures are opportunities to learn, not reasons to blame or discipline. Promote the idea that one can take certain risks to transform and that there will be problems and failures along the way. Failing fast enough will not impact the overall organization.

Institute regular meetings to talk about failures. What happened? What did you learn from it? That's the entire meeting agenda. Failing without learning is penalized; learning from failing is rewarded.

The willingness to take risks does not mean potential risk should not be assessed. The risk assessment in a product mindset environment, however, differs from one in a project mindset culture. It is meant to pinpoint risks associated with a certain action or direction and then discern those that are acceptable, even if failure could occur.

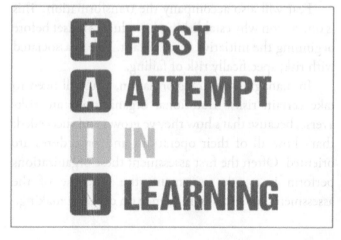

**F**IRST **A**TTEMPT **I**N **L**EARNING

# 5

# CHARTING A PATH TO THE NORTH STAR

John F. Kennedy pointed to a North Star out in space in 1962. Seven years later, the first human walked on the moon. In the 2020s, we have another influential person with a North Star in space: Elon Musk is pointing to Mars with a plan to colonize the Red Planet. In both cases, while the leaders continued to keep their people facing the North Star, they supported the experts in their organizations to chart the path.

"How will we get from here to there?" Any transformation effort must start with this question. The answer must be rooted in a clear view of what "here," the current state, looks like. It must also rest on a clearly defined "there," the target state. We talked about determining the current state in chapter two. Defining the target state, the place you will end up when the transformation initiative is complete, must be done before a path from here to there can be created.

To get the best result, target state definition needs to take place outside the boundaries of daily business. Spark and stoke imagination, challenge people's assumptions about what is feasible, get them stretching their views of what is possible.

We have accomplished this "mind-stretching" during the design thinking phase of various products—including one memorable instance in which we asked Cartus stakeholders, using Elon Musk's North Star of having one million people living on Mars by 2050, what relocating those people would look like. What would be involved? What services would Cartus need to offer that aren't being offered today? The cross-functional team members looked at this challenge with new eyes through their particular lenses. Without the restrictions and realities of their day-to-day jobs, they became more open in their thinking and more comfortable sharing aggressive ideas. This exercise contributed to a target state that colored outside the lines of norms and habits in "how we do things today."

Coloring outside the lines is essential to define a digital transformation target state. At the same time, it's important to keep both the thinking and the definition at a macro level. It would have bogged down our team if they had been allowed to go micro with concerns about the languages that all communications needed to be in, the capacity of the vessels taking people to Mars or similar details. Micro thinking tends to force the team members to re-silo themselves, thinking in terms of their functions in the company. This isn't the time for that. Micro thinking comes later; at this point, characterize the target state at a high enough level to avoid getting mired in the weeds or popping people back into their silos.

Use design thinking when defining the target state. How will the end user feel when they interact with the product/application/service? What benefit will they get from it? This is your starting point. Continue to think in terms of end user experience and value as the target state takes shape.

---

**"Think like a customer"**

*CEOs have to become learning CEOs. Not only do we have to learn the next leadership principle or the next management practice, but we also have to learn about technology and the younger generations.*

This observation is by Indra Nooyi, former CEO and board chair of PepsiCo. Over the twelve years of her tenure at the top of the corporation, Nooyi drove a major transformation of the company through strategies that were initially viewed with skepticism by others in the company. As a result of those strategies, PepsiCo experienced an 80 percent sales growth by the time she stepped down from the top office.

Nooyi put a strong focus on design thinking and user experience, which were keys to transformation. One of her mantras was "think like your customer," and she walked her talk. In the early years after taking the CEO chair, Nooyi made weekly visits to grocery stores to see PepsiCo products the way consumers saw them. She took photos of product packaging and placement and passed them along to her design staff with comments and critiques.

Thinking like a customer prompted Nooyi to lead an effort to create products that were healthier alternatives to the company's traditional offerings. Though she had board approval for the initiative, the move raised eyebrows in the industry and among stakeholders. With her oversight, the company created a line of "good for you" and "better for you" foods that could go toe-to-toe with the entrenched "fun for you" foods. She ensured that marketing and advertising were equal for both, asserting that this allowed the customer to choose without PepsiCo weighing in.

Nooyi encouraged the 26,000 people under her leadership to think beyond a single project or product. In doing so, she sowed the seed of *Josh* in the enterprise and fired up her teams to build products and solutions that people actually need.

\*\*\*

Does leadership have a role in target state definition? Yes. Keeping the North Star in front of everyone, creating *Josh* in the employees, and reminding them where the journey is headed are part of an ongoing role. In some companies, there is another more behind-the-scenes role for the executive suite. In heavily regulated industries (e.g., finance, oil and gas), leadership needs to ensure that the unfettered thinking and brainstorming by the team doesn't lead to aspects of the target state that wouldn't be acceptable to regulators. This is a practical role, one that avoids including elements in the definition that wouldn't work in the end. This is behind-the-scenes to prevent loss of team energy and motivation. The team leaders can take direction from executives and steer their members toward ideas that will work in the regulatory space. If there are team members from a governance or compliance function in the company, they can also help guide thinking into workable channels without losing team energy.

## Booyah for the Boot Camp

We offer a number of approaches in this book to shake things up, add in some chaos by design, and get employees thinking in new ways. This approach is about the boot camp mindset.

When we say boot camp, we are not talking about military boot camp, which is rigidly organized, physically and mentally grueling, and demands 24/7 duty.

We are talking about commercial boot camps, which have become a way of delivering concentrated training in a very short time. In this kind of boot camp, you don't know what will happen. You may go for, say, three weeks of supervised sessions, and while the instructors know the agenda throughout those three weeks, you have no idea. You are excited to be part of it and expect to have fun while you do a lot of work, coming out the other end with new skills and goals met.

Hold a boot camp with your transformation team. Set clear goals and create an agenda that will keep participants off-balance, challenged, and doing their best work. Design activities that will snap them out of their usual ways of looking at challenges and approaching solutions. Have participants do tasks that are not part of their daily roles.

During the design thinking session, one of the major processes is to create empathy around the user or customer who is going to use the product—for example, age, profession, and gender. The team going through the design thinking sessions should represent many teams but challenge their daily "we have always done things this way" instincts. One approach is to interchange their representation, keeping user empathy and business objectives in mind. For example, ask tech team representative to represent the legal area or vice versa. The idea here is to challenge the norm.

The time frame is up to you. It could be a weekend lockdown with a program that extends into the evening hours and participants sleep on premises. It could be a series of weekdays in the office with participants holed up in a conference room from eight to five. It could be two- or three-day events, each focused on particular outcomes. Use instructors and facilitators skilled in boot camp instruction, whether from within the company or from the outside. Create subteams and set up good-natured competitions between them.

Taking a boot camp approach with your transformation team can deliver great results. Among these:

- You will generate excitement among team members.
- The team will coalesce and bond, which is especially useful if members are from different parts of the company and have not worked together before.
- You will kick-start innovative thinking and the important "fail fast" approach that might have been unfamiliar to this point.

And among other results, your initiative will gain momentum in a short time. This will help keep the energy and excitement going, propelling the project forward.

***

The North Star differs from the target state. The North Star does not change; the target state will evolve as external and internal factors shift. In that way, our North Star metaphor is the same as the actual North Star in the sky. It doesn't change position, though the rest of its environment may shift. People can navigate by it and know where they are in relation to it. An organization's North Star operates the same way. It is the unchangeable element that teams and projects navigate by. It is the reference point that drives the direction taken.

NASA's North Star during the space program of the 1960s was getting a human to the moon. To accomplish that, the agency had to step through a series of target states—the unmanned vehicle programs, and the manned Mercury, Gemini, and Apollo programs. Musk's North Star is colonizing Mars. Between now and then, a series of target states will be achieved, like Starlink, the low orbit satellite internet company. Starlink is a target state, and the revenues the company generates will go toward achieving the North Star, which in this case is Mars.

Let's bring our examples back to Earth. A more relatable illustration is something that has become a staple of daily life: the ATM. The first ATM in the United States was unveiled at a branch of Chemical Bank in New York City in 1969. (The UK had introduced its first cashpoint two years earlier.) The capabilities of this first generation of ATMs were limited: They delivered specific amounts of cash (multiples of $20 bills) to account holders outside of regular banking hours. Fundamentally, these machines were minivaults with dispensing mechanisms.

Was the North Star for ATM developers something like, "Let's build a machine that will deliver cash?" No. Highly unlikely. The North Star was bigger than that, kind of a banking version of landing on the moon or colonizing Mars: Create an electronic system that can do the same things as a live teller. Over decades, this remained the North Star. The target state, however, evolved its definition. From the first target—dispense cash out of hours through machines located at bank branches—ATMs have significantly expanded their capabilities and locations. They are now ubiquitous, no longer tethered to branch locations. The advent of optical character recognition technologies added deposit capabilities. For a small fee, consumers can withdraw cash from non-bank ATMs or systems operated by banks where they do not have accounts.

ATMs today are closer to the electronic tellers of the North Star vision. Along the way, successive target states have been defined as technology has advanced, interbank networks have matured, and the regulatory environment has allowed additional capabilities.

Fifty years ago, consumers could only do their banking within specific hours at physical branch locations. Banking today takes place at the consumer's convenience, online or through an ATM, which now replicates the services of human tellers. The arc from then to now is one of digital transformation that has changed the consumer banking industry.

***

Charting a path to the North Star is accomplished through a series of target states. The target state is like a travel itinerary, defining the route to be taken and milestones along the way. It is not written in stone. Rather, it's an organic piece that can change when external factors affect organizational priorities. The document defining the target state doesn't have to be fully developed; in fact, it's better if it's not all polished and "final."

To create the target state, you will need to allow your cross-functional team members to re-silo themselves—not entirely, but enough to focus their particular expertise on the contribution to the definition. The connections formed during initiative design need to remain in place, and the team should continue to work together through all phases of the project.

Agility, that component of culture change and design thinking, also needs to be a component of the path to the North Star. Shifts in the market and the organization can call for a change in route. Facebook's motto in its early days was "move fast and break things." They were young, hungry, and disruptive. "Breaking things" means breaking the traditional ways of doing things, breaking mindsets, even breaking things from a customer perspective. They had no problem launching things that were not fully baked or releasing features and products that in "normal" organizations wouldn't be ready for public consumption. This wasn't a haphazard strategy; they wanted to capture early adopters and rely on those customers to provide feedback.

Time went by, and Facebook grew and grew. So did the organization's infrastructure, the number of users, and the number of employees. Maturing from a hungry start-up to an established commodity service required a change in how work got done. Word on the street is that a critical point was reached when an employee who made an update without following protocols almost took down the entire platform. This individual would have been lauded in Facebook's early days as a maverick. At the mature stage the company was now in, not so much. Understanding that a change in approach was needed, leadership modified Facebook's motto: "Move fast but with stable infrastructure."

Facebook COO Sheryl Sandberg relates another example of leading through transformation. Facebook was initially designed for desktop use. In the early 2010s, Mark Zuckerberg, recognizing the size of the mobile user market, decided that the company needed to adopt a "mobile-first" stance. He announced this at an all-hands meeting and, according to Sandberg, made a clear and compelling case for the shift in strategy. In spite of this, the next day, staff was back to business as usual, using desktop screenshots in their meeting materials. After seeing this over a few meetings, Zuckerberg pushed the company forward by saying, "'No more meetings unless you are demonstrating mobile-first in your screenshots." Sandberg asserted that, just by announcing that one directive, he created the needed shift. It wasn't easy, she recalls. Though management got totally on board with the new direction, it meant retraining a large number of engineers.

---

### Microsoft Versus Google: Process Change

Microsoft Office has been the standard suite of applications for business for nearly three decades. Since it launched in 1990, the core tools have been Word (word processor), Excel (spreadsheet), PowerPoint (presentations), and Outlook (email). Business processes in companies worldwide centered on Microsoft Office, incorporating their features into how things got done in virtually every industry. As the world moved online, the company added applications like Teams (collaboration/chat) and SharePoint (project/ team resources), transforming the entire suite into Office 365. This subscription-based, continuously updated approach to application delivery retained Microsoft's dominance. Until recently.

Google has offered tools and resources to its users almost since its inception. It formally launched Google Apps for Your Domain in 2006. The application package was renamed Google G Suite in 2016 and Google Workspace in 2020. The core tools that comprise the platform are similar to those offered by Office 365: Gmail and Calendar paralleling Outlook; Docs paralleling MS Word; Sheets paralleling MS Excel; and Slides paralleling MS PowerPoint. Google Workspace also includes collaboration tools like Drive and Chat.

Google Workplace has replaced Microsoft Office in many companies. The result has been a corresponding shift in business processes. While the fundamental actions taken in creating and sharing files didn't change, the way people engaged with the files had to change. Employees in Google Workspace companies had to learn how each of the core tools worked (not too hard, as the functions were similar to the Microsoft versions). More significantly, processes relating to how people interacted with files and with each other had to change. Document, spreadsheets, slide decks could be reviewed, commented on, and edited in real time, and people with access to those files could see comments and edits in real time.

For workers who had been "all Microsoft" for years, the use and process changes attached to Google Workspace required a mental and behavioral shift. Some found this shift easier to make than others, but in the end, the companies who now use Workspace made the move fairly easily.

The shifts that companies and employees had to make to their processes because of the move from Microsoft to Google represent those that take place in a digital transformation initiative. Applications and tools that were used before may have been fine, and processes may have been created based on those applications and tools. The transformation will shift to new applications and tools—or at least new versions of those—and new processes will need to be implemented. People will have different reactions to the change, and support mechanisms should be put in place to facilitate their adoption of the new ways, even if they initially don't see the reasons or benefits right away.

*** 

We have implied this already, but now we will say it clearly: The target state is not the same as the end state. As is true in all parts of the business, nimbleness and agility are key in a digital transformation initiative. Changes in the external market and customer behavior, shifts in corporate strategy, or, as we discuss later, unexpected and urgent demands on the company may require a redefinition of the target state. As an example, Tesla—which began life as electric car company Tesla Motors—is now as much a battery company as an automobile manufacturer. Even more drastically, Amazon—which was founded as an online counterpoint to traditional brick-and-mortar booksellers—is now a retailer of all things under the sun as well as an electronics manufacturer (e-readers and smart home devices), on-demand cloud-computing platform (Amazon Web Services), artificial intelligence pioneer (Alexa), global content creator (Prime Video) and on and on and on. Consequently, both of these companies have undoubtedly redefined their target states numerous times along the way—and, presumably, will continue to do so for as long as they hope to dominate their respective markets.

Sometimes the North Star itself changes, which shifts the transformation initiative. For example, a company operating in the business-to-business space that wants to move into the direct-to-customer space for certain products or services would define a North Star specific to the new strategy. That new North Star could impact (or prompt) a digital transformation initiative.

Building agility into the planning process is crucial in large multiyear transformation programs. External and internal situations can change fairly quickly, and the digital initiative may need to rechart the path to the North Star (or perhaps the North Star itself) more than once. There must be ways to retune and change the initiative built into the planning effort.

## A Marie Kondo Metaphor

Digital transformation often needs to be disorganized before it comes together. It is like reorganizing a house. It isn't as effective to go one room at a time as it is to just get everything together in one place, sort out the stuff that's not needed, and then rethink where the necessary stuff should go.

Marie Kondo made this approach famous through her books and television show. When it's time to work on the client's closets, she takes all the contents from every closet in the house and puts everything in one place. First, she says, sort out what is needed from what isn't needed. Then concentrate on what's needed and reorganize.

This can be intimidating for some people. Someone comes in to organize one closet in your house and says, "I'm going to help you with your closet, but first, I'm going take all the clothes out of *all* your closets and drawers and put everything in one place."

What is the likely reaction? Resistance, annoyance, perhaps even anger. Yet Marie Kondo has proven the value of her approach time after time. The ability to see everything in one place, and then have a neutral third party facilitate the reorganization, exceeds expectations.

This is "necessary chaos," and it is highly effective in a digital transformation effort. We often take a Kondo-like approach with clients: "Bring everything you know, put it on one piece of paper, and then we will re-engineer things so you can see where your biggest opportunities for transformation lie." Like Kondo, we take on processes one at a time rather than upend the whole "house." We take one process and go team by team, department by department, finding overlaps, redundancies, and unique efficiencies that weren't obvious until seeing everything in one place. Then repeat until we've tackled and reorganized the whole process.

Another aspect of Kondo's work is analogous to the *Josh* that is a vital part of digital transformation. Along with physical organization, she asserts that her efforts "spark joy" in her clients. While joy is not quite what *Josh* is about, it is about sparking excitement among team members and the employee population. Like Kondo, we've seen this effect in engagement after engagement.

# 6

# GOING FOR THE WIN

We must begin this chapter with some expectation setting. This is the point in your transformation planning where your team needs to dive into the weeds. We won't get into transactional details about how to do that dive. There are plenty of books on the market about topics like project management, design thinking, and user experience. They offer in-depth guidance for the "doingness" of creating and managing initiatives. Our intention here is to offer the level of information that a leader or executive needs to keep things moving in the right direction.

\*\*\*

In one project, we were looking at defining the product structure, and we hired high-power consultants to help define our construct. Unfortunately, the person running the project decided to micromanage the whole team: *Here's exactly how the overall structure will look; here are the tools you will use; here's step one, step two, step three;* and so on. The team spent months spinning their wheels, bogged down in the details. Milestones were not met as time was wasted. Team members fell into a sort of learned helplessness as they relied on the manager to direct them instead of moving forward on their own.

We finally had to step in with three months left on the schedule. We fired the consultants, rejiggered the team, and stepped back. "Here is the North Star we need to follow," we told the team. "We will be here as guides, and we will make sure there are guardrails in place so you don't get off track, but you need to navigate each stage of the journey in the way you see fit."

The new approach took hold big time. Granted autonomy, the team became incredibly productive. The project was completed on time with successful results

\*\*\*

The greatest strategy in the world won't lead to a successful transformation if the execution is botched. Once the groundwork has been laid, "macro" gives way to "micro," and leaders must step back to let their people do what they do best. At the same time, the role of the leadership team now gets augmented. They must continue pointing to the North Star, championing the transformation initiative, and communicating clearly to the workforce. They must also become coaches.

And yes, we did try to come up with some other metaphor than a sports team. Comparing business and sports has been used so much, it's almost a trope. The problem was that we couldn't come up with a better metaphor for leadership's role in both the early and later stages of a transformation initiative.

To wit: A basketball, baseball, football, or other sports team has a North Star that the coach points to—National championship, World Series, Super Bowl. The head coach points to the North Star, motivates the players, works with the other coaches to ensure that performance is the best it can be. Those coaches work with groups of players based on roles. When it's time for the game, the players take the field and do what's needed to win.

Similarly, while an organization's leaders also step back at this point in the transformation, they do not disengage. While the "players" on their team do what's needed for their specific roles and positions, the leaders become coaches. They track progress, and their interactions maintain motivation and correct course if needed.

In other words: Be a servant leader—and have your managers be servant leaders as well. This type of leadership puts employee (and customer) experiences ahead of profit. Servant leaders cultivate their own emotional intelligence and apply that intelligence to how they lead. They honor and welcome diversity of background and thinking, and they create both physical and psychological safety in the workplace. Career and personal growth is a priority for their employees, as is health and well-being.

Servant leaders clearly demonstrate that their employees are valued, and they openly recognize excellence in performance. Other qualities of servant leaders include:

- **Emphasis on community.** They know that mutual trust between team members is important, and they focus on fostering that trust and building community as a result.
- **Commitment to staff development.** Servant leaders sponsor personal and skill development by providing resources and budget so employees have what they need to further their goals and improve their skills.
- **Promoting continuous team learning.** They implement learning processes that allow teams to learn before, during, and after initiatives and projects to capture what works and identify what needs improvement, then share findings across the organization.
- **Adherence to persuasion.** Servant leaders manage through persuasion rather than a mandate. They build consensus to achieve buy-in.
- **Dedication to self-awareness.** They reflect on their own strengths and weaknesses and understand there are places and functions where they will make the most contributions and other places and functions that would be best filled by others.

Be a servant leader. Engage with the people and trust the processes. Make sure team members are pointing toward the North Star, then step back and allow them to proceed. As long as the team's results don't deviate from the *intent* of the strategy, even if their approach differs from what you expected, empower your people to make the decisions to achieve their ends. Don't make prescriptive demands ("Use this tool, not that tool!"); don't micromanage. Stay up to date on status, provide input and feedback when it's needed, and facilitate learning from failures. Maintain a light touch, be a servant leader, and let your people soar.

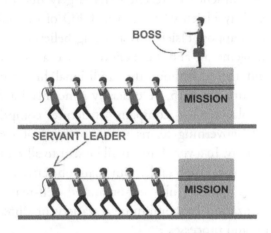

### From legacy structure to self-management

*"The best leaders are those that lead by example and are both team followers as well as team leaders. We believe that, in general, the best ideas and decisions are made from the bottom up, meaning by those on the front lines that are closest to the issues and/or the customers. The role of a manager is to remove obstacles and enable his/her direct reports to succeed. This means the best leaders are servant-leaders. They serve those they lead."*

– Tony Hsieh, *Delivering Happiness: A Path to Profits, Passion, and Purpose*

The concept of servant leadership has been in the management space for over half a century. It came to prominence in recent years largely due to the late Tony Hsieh when he was CEO of the online store Zappos. Hsieh was a strong believer in self-management, and he believed that a company could thrive without the traditional hierarchical structure. In 2015, he officially announced a shift to holacracy—a company structure comprised of self-governing teams with no shred of legacy hierarchy. In a very long email he sent to all Zappos employees, Hsieh said, "Our main objective is…to make Zappos a fully self-organized, self-managed organization by combining a variety of different tools and processes."

Though servant leadership can exist in a traditional organizational structure, the holacracy model facilitated it. Hsieh asserted that in a self-governing organization structure, servant leaders would naturally show up. There wouldn't be a management structure that conferred "leadership" onto certain people on the org chart who may or may not be leaders. Instead, leaders would be revealed as the self-managing teams in Zappos moving forward to get the work done.

Hsieh never stopped exploring alternative organizational structures in pursuit of the best way to grow as a company. Near the end of his tenure at Zappos, he moved the company to a market-based model, where teams operated much like small businesses, developing and taking products to market. As one business journalist observed, being with Tony was never boring.

Your overall approach will be appropriate to your team and company. The way forward might be to deliver results with a "fail fast" approach. Or the approach might be to arrive at a more complete result before delivering it. There's no "best" option. We have seen initiatives that were well planned and slowly executed produce the desired results. We have seen others where team members just jumped into doing what they needed to do, eventually coming out the other side with the desired results.

The approach that is "best" is specific to each company and its culture, which is why this book is not a step-by-step guide to transformation. In a more traditional, risk-oriented organization, it might be best to just jump in without a lot of planning and start doing things. If the organization is new with younger talent, the best approach may be, "Let's learn a bit and do some planning before we try to execute the initiative."

Read that paragraph again. Do you find it counterintuitive? Perhaps you assumed that the traditional organization would do best with the well-planned and executed approach. Wrong. In this scenario, it's important to create a shift to a "fail fast" approach. Remove penalties for failing, take away people's fear of those penalties, and get them comfortable with failures and learning opportunities.

The newer, young organization would thrive with the "just jump in" mindset, right? They are already a "fail fast" culture, so they're set. Wrong again. Retain the "fail fast" approach, yes, but also set up information gathering and planning at the beginning. This will teach employees when to be more deliberate and when to jump in.

In other words, run counter to the culture in the approach you take to bringing everything together and moving forward. Doing this will roil up creative chaos and keep people on their toes. They will avoid falling back into the "this is the way we've always done it" groove, whether that way has been deliberate and well-planned or the opposite.

---

### The Consequences of Thinking in Old Ways

In a previous organization, the executives had set their sights on a transformation initiative. Communication about the project trickled down to the director and senior level, but it wasn't crystal clear, and we often misunderstood their intentions. There was no *Josh*. And there definitely was none of the chaos that sparks energy and innovation.

The key concept that wasn't coming through was the need for speed. We needed to build our teams, but we didn't realize that the executives wanted us to do it quickly—go around the office, pull five or ten people, sit down, and get started.

We didn't make that leap in thinking. Instead, we did what we had always done. We figured out how many people we would need, wrote job descriptions, went through HR to post positions—the usual process.

It took time, as this kind of process always does. By the time we'd gotten our teams together, the excitement around the transformation had died out. The executives felt that we didn't understand what was needed, so they brought in consultants tasked to do whatever was needed to make things happen. They revamped the technology organization, sending some functions offshore and implementing other strategies.

By the time the consultants had done their thing, a full year had passed since the original announcement of the initiative. The actual program had not even launched yet. So much time had gone by that everyone forgot why we were even doing it.

The company did get *some* benefits from all their efforts: cheaper employees, some financial benefits, more centralization of operations. But transformation didn't happen.

Here's what we learned from this experience about implementing transformation: Move fast, get things

> done outside the usual ways, keep the excitement level high—and make sure the managers you are relying on are clear about all of it!

***

Too often, leaders and teams approach digital transformation the way they do other change management strategies: by focusing exclusively on people, processes, and technology (not necessarily in that order). A fourth consideration—the secret sauce. It's what fuels people's buy-in to transformation, and gets them actively on board.

In fact, it's so essential to the success of a transformation initiative, we are temporarily abandoning our use of the global "we" to share this story from Imran:

*I had come from a Middle Eastern country to the United States, and I had taken a lower status job to make that transition. After three and a half months at my new company, I still had no autonomy in my job. My boss told me what to do and that was that.*

*I am a programmer, and we tend to work fourteen hours a day. Even if we are with our families or spending time doing other things, our minds are always turning over problems. So I hadn't socialized much at work; I was focused on getting my work done.*

*I was excited when I first met Kader. It was at an all-hands meeting of sixty or seventy people, and he was speaking to someone who was one level higher than him. He stood up in front of everyone and said, "I'm going to do this with or without you. I'm going to do it, so you can either tell me how, or I'll figure out how to do it myself."*

*I had never seen someone speak up the hierarchy before. I knew this was a guy I wanted to work with. This was a chance for me to grow my problem-solving abilities and generally improve. I was energized by Kader's passion, and I asked around to see if I could get onto his team. And I did.*

That excitement that Imran talked about is what we call *Josh*. It is energetic, it is positive, and it's something that you want to build in the company around the digital transformation initiative.

*Josh* is the fourth factor in the equation. Think of it as the context of the whole transformation, the environment that the people, process, and technology operate in. Without it, even if everything is done right, the initiative will fail.

Before understanding how critical this piece is for success, we had more failures than successes in our projects. Using those failures as learning opportunities, we came to see that this element of excitement and motivation, *Josh*, was the missing ingredient. Since that realization, our projects have seen great success.

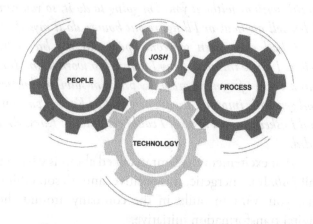

## The Black Sheep of Pixar

Pixar is a company committed to digitally transforming when they are at the top of their game. They don't wait until they've fallen behind to get disruptive. They know that it's better to transform when you're already at the top and not falling behind so you have the resources and morale—and *Josh*—supporting you.

Pixar director Brad Bird's North Star was to do something that had never been done in film animation. He assembled a team of black sheep in Pixar and sequestered this division from the rest of the company so they could create a transformation in a transformative company.

Pixar was different from the get-go. One of their biggest worries was about becoming complacent—a worry rarely found in the executive suite. When

Brad first came to Pixar, the company had made three movies—*Toy Story*, *A Bug's Life*, and *Toy Story 2*—all of them huge hits. Steve Jobs, Ed Catmull, and John Lasseter—the company cofounders—told him, "The only thing we're afraid of is complacency—thinking we have it all figured out. We want you to shake things up." Brad, who had come to the company directly from producing *Iron Giant*, which had been far less of a success than the Pixar films, was taken off guard. Getting an invitation from these three guys, with nothing but successes under their belts, to give him carte blanche to shake things up was an incredible opportunity. Literally.

Brad's first Pixar project was *The Incredibles*. In the world of animation, that was the epitome of shaking things up. Human characters with hair, water and fire with realistic motion, and a huge number of backgrounds and sets.

*Josh* was strong among the creative leaders when Brad demonstrated what we wanted. The technical people, on the other hand, balked. There was no way. It would take years and hundreds of millions of dollars to make this work. How could they possibly pull it off?

Brad's response was, "Give me your black sheep. The frustrated creative people. The technical experts whose ideas no one is listening to. The malcontents who may have one foot out the door."

In other words, he wanted a team of people who thought differently within Pixar, who swam against the current, and who had transformative ideas that were too "out there" even for a company like Pixar.

Brad asked the company leaders to let his team try crazy ideas, and he got the green light to go ahead. The black sheep got the opportunity to prove the merit of their ideas and theories.

The purists who thought that things had to be done a certain way got the rug pulled out from under them. Brad basically scared them into seeing that he would go a different (and, to them, wrong) way if they took too much time to get a particular effect via computer. Can't do the water effects through the computer? No problem, he said, I'll film a swimming pool splash and use that. Can't construct a flying saucer with computer graphics? Okay, he said, I'll film a pie plate being thrown across the screen. Brad didn't do either of these things, but taking this stand with the "in a rut" purists shook them up to the point where they saw they didn't have to make things work from every single angle in every single instance.

In Brad's view, the project wasn't a success because the team was comprised of black sheep. It was their passionate involvement and engagement—their collective *Josh*—that made the difference.

Sports (yes, those again) are full of *Josh* moments. If you have sat in the stands of a baseball game and watched your team come from behind—ninth inning, two outs, bases loaded, and a full count on the batter, who then hits it out of the park to win the game—you have experienced *Josh*. Your excitement is amplified by the people around you, and it builds into a heady sense of accomplishment and deep satisfaction.

In a company, leadership creates *Josh*. How it is created varies from company to company and leader to leader. It can be sparked by an attitude like Kader's when Imran first met him: "I will do this. I don't care what anyone says." It can arise from the strength of the leader's personality, like the example of Elon Musk we talked about earlier. *Josh* is rooted in a clear view of "why we're doing this," which gets people rallied around the initiative and rooting for its success.

*Josh* is not traditional, meaning it isn't part of the usual approach of bringing in consultants and other third parties to work the transformation. They try to follow traditional processes and procedures, talk to employees, and get feedback—all the stuff that's supposed to create buy-in. Instead of buy-in, things get diluted. No excitement, no *Josh*. It's not something you can pay a consultant to create. It is generated by you and passed on throughout the organization.

\*\*\*

What does success look like? How will we know the right results have been delivered?

These are questions to answer during this consolidation phase. Though the North Star is the ultimate goal, each target state along the way will have its signs of success in execution. NASA's program succeeded when Neil Armstrong left his footprint on the moon. Between Kennedy's announcement and "The Eagle has landed," the Mercury, Gemini, and Apollo programs each had different definitions of success. Further, the different teams and undertakings that comprised each of those "umbrella" programs had target states to execute against and definitions of what success looks like.

So, what does success look like in a business transformation effort? The answer depends on the goals of the target state and the North Star. Success might be identical to the target state goal; for example, deliver a quality product within six months where the North Star is to establish a new value proposition to customers and prospects. It's important to define success—how will you and your team know that you've achieved what you set out to achieve? Be detailed and, if possible, quantitative in the definition.

One way to define success is to work backward from the target state goal or the North Star itself. Begin at the date of delivery/implementation and track backward: What needs to happen before delivery, then what needs to happen before that, and before that, and so on. You work backward through time to the present. There will be lots of branches as you move along, and there will be holes that you can go back and fill in when they become apparent. There will also be relationships and dependencies between branches, and some may not have been obvious before doing the exercise. Without question, this activity can be illuminating. It will allow a tremendous amount of preflight action that stacks the deck in your favor.

Alternatively, worst case, you may find once you've completed the backward construction of the anticipated way forward that this way forward will *not* work to get you to success; you'll have to take a different approach. Even this worst case is immensely useful. How much better to realize before you start that the way you thought it would go won't work! Time saved, money saved, and people spared a lot of effort that must be left behind.

\*\*\*

*Execution* is the key word here. Coming into this phase of the transformation, focus has been on defining, planning, motivating. Defining the North Star, crafting strategies for capturing hearts and minds, infusing the company culture with a product mindset and fail fast approach—all of that, as important as it is, means nothing without execution. It just sits on a hard drive or white board somewhere. Execution is the lever that creates transformation.

Execution is all about being specific in the context of the target state and North Star. What does success look like? How are we going to get there? What resources do we need? What knowledge can we tap into that will help us succeed? Your team needs to answer these and other questions in detail, and you and your leadership team need to understand and ratify those answers.

Execution of the phases of a transformation journey can look like this:

- Do it in chunks
- Do it faster
- Learn from it
- Get feedback
- Improve it
- Repeat

This cycle is a big improvement over the noniterative approach. Say you have to deliver a new product in six months with all kinds of bells and whistles. This is your target state on the path to the North Star. Start from scratch and move through the execution phases above for the first three months. The team gains experience and knowledge through feedback from external and internal customers. Use the remaining three months to go through successive fail-fast executions of the *Do-Learn-Feedback-Improve* cycle to make a much better product. Success: The product is ready in six months. Of even more significance, the product is better than it would have been with a single long (project mindset) execution.

Process always lags behind people and technology. It is often weirdly dear to people, because it is rooted in the company evolution mythology. "This is how we do things around here. This is what makes the company the way it is. This is what makes us successful." Often people don't want to change a process because they think it will change the company in undesired ways. The resistance to process change is usually there simply because people are comfortable with the way things are. The processes are familiar; they have mastered them. They don't see a compelling reason to upend things and take on the discomfort and time to learn something new.

People can also conflate processes with their jobs. *Without such and such a process that I've always done, my job will change or, worse, might go away entirely. My value as an employee is on the line (in my mind).* The logic goes something like, "This is how I do my job to achieve the outcomes that I was hired to achieve, and if you take away this process, you take away my ability to create those outcomes. Then you have no reason to keep me employed here." The approach to remove this obstacle is to emphasize (as often as needed) that the job is to produce X, not follow a specific set of steps to produce X.

People might not even be able to articulate why they are resistant. It ultimately comes down to, "But that's not how we do it," or, "But we've never done it that way." This is not at all objective, yet we hear this or something like it repeatedly as an explanation for why someone or something shouldn't change. The world is constantly changing and so is their business environment; if you've never done it before, now might be a good time to start.

Some people also connect processes with quality. They think that if they follow established processes, the outcome will have a higher quality. We've seen this operate as a feature of culture; as soon as you ask something about process, even to simply gain knowledge, the reaction is, "You obviously don't care about quality. This has been going on for years and years, and our quality is so good because we follow this specific process."

People who connect processes with quality need to be coached to understand that the two are independent. It's not that processes don't have an impact on quality— of course they do, or they wouldn't be in place. It's that a specific set of processes is not the only avenue to ensure high quality. It's important that people realize this, and it may take a big change in their assumptions and viewpoints to get there.

The blocks you may encounter with employees' attitudes toward process is one reason why focusing on people first is so important. Continuing to point to the North Star and capturing hearts and minds have to precede everything else. If you try to address process first, it can be a recipe for failure because of unexpected emotional attachment. Unless you and your team have articulated the North Star and done the groundwork to capture hearts and minds, you can't succeed if the stakeholders you've identified in your heatmaps and other findings are mired in the current process. They need to be ready, eager even, to shake things up.

Readiness to shake things up, to add in chaos by design, frees employees to think differently about their jobs. It may be as small as changing from an analog to a digital tool. Or it could be as big as a full pivot in their area of focus to acknowledge the new reality and see that the work still leverages strengths they have even if the new reality includes components that weren't part of their previous core role.

\*\*\*

Your people, processes, and technology comprise an ecosystem. Each element affects the other, and a change to one affects the other two. As you get into the digital transformation initiative, there are some outcomes that may not be predictable. For example, in application development where a new process is implemented, you don't know ahead of time whether you will reduce or increase cycle time. It depends on your ecosystem and how the people and technology elements relate to or react to the new process.

As an example, at Cartus the increased pace of application development has decreased cycle time. Within four months, we had our first MVP (minimally viable product) application; within two more months, we had our second application. Outstanding results for a large organization.

On the other hand, at a large banking institution where we worked previously, the time to deliver the first application was a year and a half. That did not mean we were doing something wrong or something bad. The organization's structure—its ecosystem—was so complicated that it took some time for the first true result of the transformation to become evident. Once that first result was produced, we got into a rhythm of application development and delivery, and cycle time accelerated significantly.

In a digital transformation, technology is the critical element. In the majority of organizations we have worked with, there is a particular technology configuration that everyone is used to and that processes are built around. It is important to evaluate the technology configuration and compare the vision, the North Star, with what you have in place. Given where you want to go, whatever that North Star is, does the current technology configuration support getting there? Actually, whether you engage in a digital transformation or not, this is a question to ask periodically, at least every five years.

Let's say you are using Microsoft Azure, and things are fine. But in thinking about transformation, you are considering shifting to Google Cloud. One reason to shift (and this is an example; you can ask this question about any platform shift) is that the change from Microsoft to Google will require a change in the people and process elements of your ecosystem. There is chaos in that change, and that can be a daunting consideration. However, if you stay with Microsoft, people will go back to their old way of doing things with the same processes as before. Shifting to Google or another cloud platform means that people need to make their brains do a little more work to solve challenges in the new system. Chaotic? Yes, at first, but well worth it in the long run.

If we don't force people to use a different technology to solve the same problem, they will go back to their daily routine. This applies to your developers, technology experts, architects, and everyone else. Ask, "Why not use something completely different to force ourselves to think differently?" If, say, your organization always uses Java as your programming language, maybe you tell your team, "Don't use Java, use Angular to do the same thing." That change to the ecosystem will make your people shift their thinking, which is a good thing.

The process element of the ecosystem will also need to "think" differently. Uber is an example of this. Uber said, "We know that you want to move a person from one place to another." But they asked a fundamental question that changed thinking: "Why do I need to always have a Crown Vic as a car? Why can't I use my own car?" That question caused ripples in the ecosystem. For example, If they are going to use their personal car, how do we make sure that car works? Taxi operators used to do inspections every month and drivers carried a certificate of safety, implying that the car you were in was safe enough to drive you around. So Uber had to come up with processes that ensured that their drivers' cars were safe.

One caveat about the people element of the ecosystem. People can get frustrated. A good example is learning a new language. If you have ever been in another country and immersed in that new language, it can be a very frustrating experience. What are routine and simple tasks at home, like ordering a meal or asking directions, can become difficult and stressful in the new environment. If you continue to spend time in that environment, your mastery of the language will improve and you will find it easier to converse and get things done.

In the developer example above, you have asked your team to essentially use a different language to get their tasks done so that they will think differently. You might find, though, that you get diminishing returns from mandating the change from Java to Angular. Frustration, even anger, can impede progress and prevent results. This is counterproductive. The reason for the change was to prompt your people to think differently and come at their work in a new way. If after a period of time using Angular, you see that your developers are more upset than productive, balance your strategy. You may say, "You know what? Leave Angular; let's go back to Java. At least now you have had the opportunity to think a little differently."

There are a couple of metaphors to think about when it comes to your people and fostering their approach to transformation. First is a dog with a curly tail—an Akita or Samoyed. If you take the tail and straighten it out, it will stay straight as long as you hold onto it. Let go, and it curls right back up. You could stand over your developers and hound them to think differently every second of the day, and they might do so while you're there. But if they remain in the same environment without your constant reminder, they'll revert to their old ways of thinking and working. Shake them up, make the path of least resistance the direction they need to go. Recall the story about Facebook's shift to a mobile-first company. Zuckerberg didn't stand over people and hammer away at them to make such a fundamental shift. He simply said "no more meetings" until the way people viewed their work changed.

On the other hand, think of a rubber band. You can pull that rubber band to a longer length, and as long as you hold onto it, it will stay longer. Let go, and it will snap back to its regular size. This is the same thing as that Akita tail. As long as you hold onto that new "rubber band length" in your people, they will think differently. Stop reminding them, let go of the rubber band, and they will revert. The difference with this metaphor is that if you stretch the rubber band too far, it will break, and that's no good either. You need to see how far you can stretch your people to think differently, but if you see by their behavior that you have stretched them too far, allow them to snap back, even if only for a little while. They will have experienced a new way of thinking, and taking the pressure off could be a greater benefit in the long run.

***

Part of transforming your ecosystem is breaking down the walls, both figuratively and literally. Think about creating a physical space conducive to collaboration. Companies with agile cultures have spaces called "communities" and "neighborhoods." A larger team is a community; neighborhoods are small teams within the community. These companies created physical workspaces that reflect this way of collaborating.

Another type of physical change is the virtual office. Even before the coronavirus pandemic, there were companies that were 100 percent virtual. People worked from home (or wherever they wanted to) and collaborated through virtual conferencing, chat rooms, and online interactions in real time or asynchronously. Use of this type of workspace increased because of COVID-19, and in many cases, it may stay in place. It is important to create the same community/neighborhood experience for your teams. This can be done in a variety of ways while keeping everyone remote.

***

As a leader, going for the win means that once the path to the North Star has been charted, you need to step back and let your people do the work. Maintain oversight, be the "guard rail" that keeps them focused on the right things, and make the changes in your ecosystem that are consistent with the transformation. Stretch your people to think and work differently, but balance that demand so the rubber band doesn't break. Make sure the physical or virtual space in which your teams work supports collaboration.

Your leadership, along with your people, will ensure the transformation puts the company in a whole new place.

# OF SPECIAL NOTE: POSITIONING FOR URGENT TIMES

Leaders creating strategic plans and finalizing budgets to prepare for 2020 had no way of knowing those plans and budgets would turn out to be cards in a game of "52 Pickup" by March of that year. The COVID-19 pandemic caused abrupt shifts in priorities.

- Product strategy gave way to reactive pandemic measures
- Employee safety became an urgent priority
- Shifts in tactics and strategies had to remain aligned with the organization's mission

There is no arguing that COVID-19 had a drastic effect on variables. One huge example is the sudden need for employees to become remote workers. This meant more than just having laptops they could take home. They needed ways to virtually communicate with each other, send materials securely, and access the assets and artifacts they needed to do their jobs. Businesses that already operated virtually in whole or part were way ahead of the curve, because they had the technology and processes in place to make the needed pivot.

## Zoom and the Pandemic: Serving Customers in Need

Videoconferencing platforms have cropped up in numbers over the past couple of decades. Zoom is a relative newcomer, but it is now dominating the space.

Though Zoom may have become dominant in its market at some point if life had proceeded on its pre-2020 path, the COVID-19 pandemic rocketed it to a top spot for personal and business communication use. While the net effect is great for the company, the road to dominance has not been smooth. In common with many enterprises across all business sectors, Zoom had to move fast to accommodate the new environment in which its employees and customers worked and played.

Many leaders will recognize the challenges Zoom encountered and the measures it took to address them. Zoom's primary challenge, unsurprisingly, was a massive and rapid rise in demand for its services: The user base grew by 3,000 percent in four months, from 10 million in December 2019 to 300 million in April 2020. In the early days of lockdowns and work-from-home mandates, the company got bad press because of security breaches that resulted in "Zoombombings." The online harassment took leaders off-guard. Zoom had been primarily a business videoconferencing platform and had worked with customer IT departments to ensure it met security protocols. With a huge influx of individual customers and organizations that lacked digital savvy, Zoom was vulnerable to incursions. It rapidly addressed the issue to protect its clients' online meetings, and it continues to strengthen the platform's security.

With such massive growth in such a short time, infrastructure challenges also presented themselves. In the pandemic's early days, platform crashes occurred relatively frequently. To minimize the chances for continued outages, Zoom engineers added servers to all seventeen data centers to accommodate dramatically increased volume. Further, the company expanded its cloud infrastructure through Microsoft Azure and Amazon Web Services.

Zoom also significantly accelerated its hiring to quickly bring in the skill sets needed to meet the new market challenges. For example, a report in May 2020 indicated that the company had hired 500 developers in their Phoenix data center in a single week to help keep up with rising demand.

Despite early hiccups, Zoom is now the go-to virtual meeting, conference, and classroom for users around the world as COVID-19 continues to demand a different way of communicating. One of the surest signs of its position in the business world today is that, just as "Google" became a verb for any internet search, "Zoom" has become a verb for a virtual meeting. And like Xerox and Kleenex, Zoom has replaced more generic nouns describing the product!

Many companies on the verge of launching or in the middle of digital transformation shifted into warp drive in response to the demands that the pandemic placed on them. Some enterprises did not restrategize or modify their roadmaps. Instead, they *accelerated* what they already had in place. It wasn't a matter of frantically putting together a new roadmap. It was, "We already had a product roadmap, and when COVID-19 happened, we reprioritized what was already there and moved money and other resources to align with the change."

Jeff Lawson, CEO of Twilio—which offers software to allow developers to include communication capabilities in their applications—noted the digital acceleration in his area of technology. Twilio was well-positioned to help thousands of companies quickly shift operations and interactions to virtual workplaces, so Jeff and his organization saw a close-up view of digital change. A survey conducted by Twilio examining pandemic-related business adaptations reported that digital communications strategies—initiatives originally slated to be long-term undertakings—accelerated by an average of six years. Six years! Lawson asserts that *digital acceleration* (rather than digital transformation) is the name of the game now that companies have met the need to transform because of COVID-19.

The COVID-19 pandemic experience underlines the need for any company to emergency-proof its business. A company needs to be able to turn on a dime and accelerate transformation in the right areas when something comes out of nowhere to turn everything upside down.

### The Case for Transformation NOW

US Foods is one of the largest food distributors in the US. The company offers its services to restaurants, the healthcare industry, and other sectors that offer food service.

When COVID-19 hit, US Foods had to rethink everything. Their production lines were impacted because of the six-foot safe distance requirement. For example, as meat came down the conveyor belt, two people caught the meat. They stood next to each other about two feet apart. With the six-foot separation requirement, the $3.2 billion machinery had to be modified. Multiply this across all the company's operations—US Foods faced an extreme challenge.

Fortunately, the company had experience with transformation and was prepared to pivot. Several years previously, US Foods had faced another challenge. At that time, it was essentially a logistics vendor providing food to corporations—one of many similar companies in that space. Recognizing that they could only compete on quality or price and that the scenario wasn't sustainable, leadership considered how to differentiate the company in the market.

The key realization was that they weren't primarily in the food provision business; they were a data collector and aggregator. This supported a deep level of insight into their customers' industries. US Foods pivoted from "food supplier" to "analyst/consultant" providing meaningful knowledge to companies that helped decision-making and strategy creation.

Having transformed themselves already, US Foods was well-positioned to respond rapidly to the changes brought about by the COVID-19 pandemic. They shifted their focus to what food service organizations needed to do right NOW—i.e., pivot to takeout and delivery, protect employees, and prepare to reopen in a COVID-19 environment. Their website presented a compelling message right up front: RECOVER. RESTART. REOPEN. The site spotlighted products needed in the new normal like face masks and takeout containers and showcases a section with a wide range of content and resources to help food-service organizations succeed.

> The US Foods story demonstrates the value of transforming the organization before an emergency strikes. When the pandemic occurred, the company culture was already tuned up. Rethinking operations and designing solutions that customers needed were rapidly accomplished.

***

COVID-19 is a recent and extreme example of an emergency that requires a fast response from businesses, but it's not the only one. Natural disasters like hurricanes, earthquakes, floods, and wildfires are other emergencies that can impact companies and their communities. Business continuity planning helps to a degree, but it focuses mainly on the technology aspect of keeping work going. Emergency proofing needs to be far more comprehensive to allow a company to accelerate in the right areas when an immediate pivot is needed.

COVID-19 forced every company to transform in different ways, and digital transformation is one of those ways. It is not an option anymore, and many of the changes that companies made will stay in place going forward. It is the only choice for future success. The strategies we offer in this book around digital transformation can also be applied to emergency-proof the company. With a commitment to digital transformation, a clearly defined way forward spanning two or three years, and a workforce and culture that

abounds in *Josh*, if the need to accelerate arises, a
company is in a good position to spring into action.

---

### A Pizza Poster Child

Domino's Pizza could be the poster child of digital
transformation, especially regarding the impact that
such transformation has on customer experience.
At its nadir in 2008, the company launched a
multifaceted effort to turn things around. Besides
improving food quality and expanding its menu,
Domino's invested in technologies that fostered
innovation in product delivery, franchisee support,
and customer engagement.

In a highly effective approach, Domino's executives
sponsored and supported the initiative, which:

- Set a North Star of embracing digital
  innovation to deliver quality product
  through any ordering mechanism a
  customer wished to use
- Completely overhauled its company culture
- Focused on the customer experience
  in terms of food quality and ordering
  mechanisms
- Created a more robust internal IT function
  that could support digital innovation
- Closely coupled the IT and marketing
  functions to allow rapid collaboration and
  iteration

- Developed Pulse, its proprietary point-of-sale computer system to simplify franchisee operations and inventory management
- Launched Pizza Tracker, allowing customers to track orders online
- Expanded ordering and tracking capabilities with an iPhone app
- Continued to expand the range of devices customers could use for ordering and tracking, including Twitter, Slack, and smart TVs

Domino's has invested in its workforce; today, approximately half of its headquarters staff works in software and analytics. The company has also invested in artificial intelligence and cognitive technologies to further improve customer engagement and experience. In the "cool" category, it is the first company to deliver pizza by drone.

The transformation initiative began and is sustained at the top. Domino's executives set the North Star, articulated strategies, plans, and progress, and ensured that their teams had the skills and resources needed to pursue agile processes emphasizing innovation and the customer.

Domino's reached a big milestone less than ten years after the initiation of their digital transformation: in 2017, the company passed Pizza Hut to become the largest pizza company in the world.

When the COVID-19 pandemic hit, Domino's was among the companies best positioned to weather the crisis successfully. There was no need for acceleration because the company already had the right technologies in place—contactless delivery, touchless transactions, even robotics. With its digital and agile culture, Domino's was able to adapt quickly to the sudden change in daily life brought about by lockdowns and general consumer cautiousness—no pivot required!

Domino's story demonstrates the value of digital transformation. Such transformation is not only of high business value in the best of times; it also prepares an enterprise to continue operating—an even come out ahead—in the worst of times.

***

"What will we do if an emergency hits?" This is a question worth considering and, if needed, acting on before all hell breaks loose. Though emergencies, by definition, come out of nowhere, anticipating possible effects can allow rapid response if a crisis does occur. This is often referred to as a "pre-mortem," in which companies or project teams evaluate and plan for worst case scenarios before they occur.

Acceleration is part of emergency response. When a dire event occurs, a business must accelerate in all areas. Think about how and where you will accelerate if an urgent need arises. Let's chunk it down into logical categories.

**Data.** Go back and review your business capabilities map and heatmap. In case of emergency, do you have the right capabilities in place? Are they "green?"

**North Star.** Would your North Star need to change? How might it need to change, and how does that affect your transformation work?

**Roadmap.** How might your roadmap need to change under emergency conditions? Are there opportunities to accelerate the roadmap or switch certain features or products earlier than planned? What would it take to do that? Would you need to hire additional talent? For what skill sets? Would other resources be needed?

**Market.** Would you be able to pursue different markets? Emergency situations can drastically change daily life and, by extension, buyer behavior. If, for example, your company serves a B2B market, do you have options that would allow you to enter a B2C market? Look at your competitors and alliances. Are there competitors that can become allies in an emergency? How would that look?

**People.** Business continuity has been a feature of strategic planning for some time. The focus of business continuity, though, is often on technology assets rather than human assets. The rise of COVID-19 spotlighted the need to address "worker continuity," ensuring that employees can work safely in unusual conditions for prolonged periods if necessary. If another situation arises where furloughs are required, how can you take care of your people effectively? What about hiring?

Traditional hiring processes take too long. If you need to bring in new people, how will you do that?

**Process.** How might your business processes need to change? When the COVID-19 pandemic struck, employees were suddenly required to work from home. Companies that already had remote work processes in place adapted with ease, while those that had "everyone must be onsite" mantras had to scramble. Can your processes, procedures, and policies accommodate an external crisis?

**Technology.** Beyond a business continuity plan, how can your technology infrastructure be configured to support rapid response to an emergency? For example, do you have the components in place that will allow employees to work virtually securely?

Having gone through those categories, now answer this question: Can you put the strategies you've identified into play *now* rather than waiting for the anvil to drop? If you can make those changes now, you will be in better shape to deal with disaster.

One final category must be scrutinized, and it impacts all the other categories. Setting aside contingency funds as a percent of revenue is a common practice across many business sectors. The important question in our post-COVID-19 world is, "Are we setting aside sufficient funds to meet the demands of a sudden crisis?" If, like Domino's, you are already well-entrenched in digital transformation, the answer may be yes. Or if, like Zoom, you are positioned to serve the urgent needs of your customers (and therefore can easily obtain additional funds from investors or bank loans), the answer might also be yes. But if rapid response will be needed to keep the business running, you'll need the money to make it happen.

After thinking through all the categories above, assess your contingency allocation. What financial resources would be needed to address an emergency? What would be available given the current budget? If additional funds needed to be allocated, pursue strategies like harvest and reinvest to pump up the amount. Do you need funding from outside sources? If so, what are those sources, and how should you pursue them to ensure that you will have what you need if the time comes.

\*\*\*

Essentially, there is one sure way to position for urgent times: digital transformation. Shifting culture, operations, and mindsets to "all digital, all the time" are strategies that will keep you competitive—even dominant—in your market. Beyond that, making that fundamental shift embeds agile and customer-focused approaches throughout the enterprise. As a result, everyone is light on their feet, able to accelerate where needed and pivot quickly when circumstances demand.

Even after digital transformation is underway, don't let up. Make data gathering a standard activity, review your roadmap regularly, and quickly adjust to shifts in your internal and external environments. Continue focusing on servant leadership and providing the resources, processes, and technologies that help your people to grow and in turn grow the business.

Our advocacy of acceleration in digital transformation is not limited to dire emergencies; in our collective opinion, it is part of the foundation of digital transformation. We urge you to make speed and its first derivative "the way we do things around here." Go faster on that ongoing journey and keep increasing the rate at which you go faster. Among other benefits, it will keep your *Josh* fed and healthy and turn innovation into a virtuous cycle. And it will keep you at the leading edge of digital evolution.

Cultivate a transformation mindset, make it part of the company DNA. You will be positioned to thrive in good times and survive well in urgent times.

# CONCLUSION

As we are near the end of the book, it's important to remind you that this is an idea book, not a step-by-step manual or cookbook for creating digital transformation. Each company is different, and leadership must determine the best way forward. We hope that you will incorporate the ideas and insights we've shared here into your efforts.

Now is also the time for a confession (or, if we're being honest, a humblebrag).

**We are walking, talking, breathing creators of *Josh*.**

All three of us are steeped in that all-important fourth dimension, the spark that lights up transformation. If we were superheroes, we'd have big **J**'s on our chests.

We make our *Josh* contagious whenever possible. For us, digital transformation is never about merely catching up. Many executives we have worked with started out saying, "We need our technology to catch up with our competitors'." Boring. We have to work to keep our eyes from rolling. In a presentation about Google's natural language processing tool we delivered to a group of sales and account managers, we asserted, "We're not here to catch up to current technology, folks. We are here to interrupt, to *disrupt* technology."

That stuck with people and motivated them. Why wouldn't it? Catching up is pretty ho-hum. Disrupting technology? Now that's exciting, contagious even. That's *Josh*!

We are passionate about the transformation part of digital transformation. It can be hard for people to wrap their heads around what that actually means. It's metamorphosis—an end state that is impossible to predict by looking at the current state. A person unaware of the Lepidoptera lifecycle would never look at a caterpillar and predict "butterfly." That worm-like insect making its way along a branch has nothing about it that says "diaphanous wings and nectar-sipping proboscis."

We are excited about looking at current states and asking ourselves and our clients, "What does the butterfly state look like? What end state can we achieve that most people can't imagine today?" We advocate disruption, because we know that the energy and innovation it releases can create that unimagined state, one that could not have been predicted initially.

Another aspect of transformation that drives us is the demand for quality. Much of the buying population today is a digital native. They were born into a technological world, and they rely on technology in every aspect of their lives. Following generations will be even more immersed in digital tools and capabilities.

An effect of technology immersion is an increasingly high demand for quality in their products. Design thinking and product mindset, therefore, must emphasize quality assurance in product development.

This also applies to "products" like internal infrastructure and applications for employee use.

We do recognize that quality can be in the eye of the beholder. Our approach to this reality during a transformation is to keep asking, "Can we maintain a quality level that will work for everyone?" This is another motivator for us; it's a puzzle we love solving.

*** 

What does the digital future look like? Technology continues to evolve in constantly amazing directions.

Travel west on this planet, and there is always more west to go. Technology evolution is similar: No matter what new technology or digital capability shows up, there is more on the horizon. We are excited about the near horizon developments and the technological capabilities that are so "far horizon" that they seem like science fiction.

The seeds of the future are planted in soil that is data. Most technology innovations have centered on data over the past ten years or more. Collecting it, storing it, analyzing it, moving it. The Internet of Things? Rooted in data. Artificial intelligence? Ditto. Robotics? Yeah, data (no relation to the *Star Trek: Next Generation* android, though he was aptly named).

We are now at the threshold of a new relationship with data: Using it to predict and prescribe. Predictive analytics has already established itself in the business world. From monitoring the status of oil wells out in the middle of nowhere to considering the next product launch, the ability to analyze data to predict—in these examples, how long a drill bit will last or how a particular demographic will respond—is current state or target state for many companies.

Prescriptive analytics is about what to do when the predicted situation occurs. It moves systems toward self-sufficiency, where issues could be predicted and resolved without human intervention. In our remote oil well, for example, prescriptive analytics could indicate a specific automated workstream when the drill bit gets to a particular condition. This is a primitive example; it would still take a human somewhere far away in a centralized operations location to push a button to activate the workstream. But it's on the road to much more. Prescriptive analytics will become an integral part of robotic operations of all kinds. It would certainly be part of Musk's planned voyage to Mars. Closer to home, we will see a wide range of self-sufficient machines in our homes, offices, and factories.

Prescriptive analytics is part of the near horizon of technology evolution. It's coming, and sooner than you might think. Are you ready for it? If not, the time for digital transformation is now. If you fail to do what's needed to put your business squarely into the digital world, you will end up like the buggy whip manufacturers who refused to see that the automobile would take over or like Blockbuster when Netflix came along.

\*\*\*

On the far horizon of technology evolution, bio enhancement is an area that fascinates us. There are companies working on brain-machine interfaces where the technology is placed inside the human body. There are so many possibilities for this application, like treating chronic conditions and mitigating or even eliminating disabilities. Another aspect is human augmentation, like enhancing brain operation so a person could synthesize far more data than would be possible on their own. Extrapolating even further, there could conceivably be a time when technology-enhanced humans are connected to each other through hybrid digital-neural networks—a literal peer-to-peer network.

\*\*\*

John F. Kennedy had the moon. Elon Musk has Mars. You have your North Star. Start digital transformation now, and find *Josh* in the knowledge that it will be a never-ending journey of discovery and improvement.

# ABOUT THE AUTHORS

**Kader Sakkaria** serves as the Chief Digital and Technology Officer at Ruffalo Noel Levitz (RNL). Prior to joining RNL, Kader oversaw strategic technology and digital transformation initiatives across Cartus and Realogy Leads Group. Previously, Kader was the head of business, technology, and portfolio management at BMO Harris Bank, and he has led technology initiatives for Fortune 500 and other companies such as Deloitte, Accenture, TransUnion, StateFarm, HighMark, US Foods, and Ryder Logistics. Kader holds a pending patent for a "Method and System for Estimating Relocation Costs" and serves on the board of directors for Naperville Community Television (NCTV17).

**Imran Karbhari** is VP of Technology Transformation & Strategic Initiatives at Realogy. He has led large-scale technology initiatives and digital transformation practices for companies in the United States and abroad. Imran is known as a champion for introducing new, leading-edge technologies to the organizations he calls home.

**Trevor Macomber** is a writer and marketing executive from Connecticut, where he lives with his wife and children. He has led global branding, marketing, and communications efforts for more than a dozen product launches and other go-to-market campaigns during the course of his company's digital transformation journey. *Chaos By Design* is his first book, though not his last. He is exceptionally lucky, and he knows it.

https://www.chaosbydesign.com/free

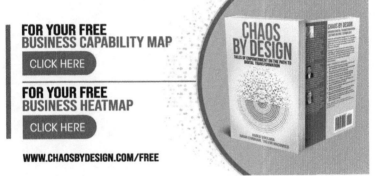

https://www.chaosbydesign.com/free